ACCIDENTS IN NORTH AMERICAN MOUNTAINEERING

VOLUME 8 • NUMBER 2 • ISSUE 55

2002

THE AMERICAN ALPINE CLUB
GOLDEN

THE ALPINE CLUB OF CANADA
BANFF

© 2002 The American Alpine Club, Inc.

ISSN   0065-082X

ISBN   0-930410-92-0

Manufactured in Canada

Published by
The American Alpine Club, Inc.
710 Tenth Street, Suite 100
Golden, CO 80401

Cover Illustration
Hoping to cinch the Girdle Traverse (5.10R), Joshua Tree National Park, California.
Photograph by Bennett Barthelemy

CONTENTS

SAFETY COMMITTEES 2001

The American Alpine Club

Aram Attarian, John Dill, Mike Gauthier, Daryl Miller,
Jeff Sheetz, and John E. (Jed) Williamson *(Chair)*

The Alpine Club of Canada

Helmut Microys, Peter Amann, Peter Roginski,
Simon Ruel, Murray Toft *(Chair)*

ACCIDENTS IN
NORTH AMERICAN MOUNTAINEERING
Fifty-Fifth Annual Report of the Safety Committees
of The American Alpine Club and The Alpine Club of Canada

This is the fifty-fifth issue of *Accidents in North American Mountaineering* and the twenty-fourth issue in which The Alpine Club of Canada has contributed data and narratives.

Canada: This was the year of the stranded climber in Canada. Four of the accidents reported in this book, plus a few others not reported here, involved climbers who got in over their heads and could no longer move up or down the mountain. The good news in these incidents is that there were no physical injuries. Climbers are advised to collect as much information about their intended route as possible before setting out to ensure that they have the skills and equipment to finish the route. The information in a guidebook is not sufficient in many cases. Other information sources include alpine journals, other climbers, park wardens, and even the internet. All climbers should remember that rescuers put their lives at risk each time they respond to a call for help from a mountain side.

There were many accidents, particularly in British Columbia, that are not reported in this book due to lack of information. Because of financial cutbacks in the B.C. government, we were not able to obtain reports from B.C. Provincial Parks. There were three climbing related deaths on the Squamish Chief for which we have no information. If anyone has knowledge of a climbing accident, you are encouraged to report it to the Editor. You may prevent someone else from suffering the same mistake.

We would like to express our gratitude to the following individuals who contributed to the Canadian section of this year's book: Marc Ledwidge, Lisa Paulson, Burke Duncan, David Henderson, Rick Staley, Ken Wiley, Ian Hyslop, Terry Taylor, Luther McLain, Rob Maiman, Doug Fulford, Rupert Wedgewood, Andrea Lines, Rob Owens, Sandy Sauer and Don Serl. Thanks also to those who fortunately either had nothing to report or who provided information that was not included in this year's book.

United States: Fatalities were at the lowest number (16) for the last 20 years. The average for this time period is 26, with the highest number at 43. Compared to hiker, hunter, skier, and other backcountry incidents, the climbing population fares well. There were fewer costly rescues this year as well. It is important to emphasize this fact again, as the question of who should pay for mountain rescue is very much in the news.

As Mike Gauthier, Chief Climbing Ranger for Mount Rainier National Park has pointed out, "As a group, mountain climbers aren't the most expensive to rescue." It is lost hikers and hunters who have achieved this distinction. Public Law 106-486, authored by Alaskan Senator Frank Murkowski, requires the

Park Service to suggest ways to recover the costs of emergency evacuations. The new congressional report may recommend that climbers on Mount McKinley be forced to carry insurance and agree to carry the costs of rescue. This could set a precedent for other parks where there is a lot of climbing activity.

The climbing community is in general agreement that the issue needs to be resolved in a manner that does not discriminate against one group in this regard. The debate continues and is often fueled by a climbing accident that becomes a media event.

Patterns to notice for this year include the number of falls made more severe by inadequate protection—either because of not enough protection being placed or because it "failed" when a fall occurred. I try to avoid the use of the word "failed," because it implies that a protection device broke, when what actually happened is that it (or they) were improperly placed. Another common cause for falls being more severe is an inadequate belay, usually due to a poor anchoring system or improper technique.

A third category to look at when reading the narratives is the number of handholds and footholds that "broke off," resulting in considerable falls. These examples provide a good reminder for one of the first lessons learned as a climber: Test all holds on any rock that has cracks or evidence of loose rocks—no matter what the size.

In addition to the Safety Committee, we are grateful to the following—with apologies for any omissions—for collecting data and helping with the report: Hank Alicandri, Micki Canfield, Ron Cloud, Jim Detterline, Bob Freund, Al Hospers, Mark Magnuson, Tom Moyer, Leo Paik, Steve Rollins, Steven Schaefgen, Robert Speik, all individuals who sent in personal stories, and, of course, George Sainsbury.

John E. (Jed) Williamson
Managing Editor
7 River Ridge Road
Hanover, NH 03755
e-mail: jedwmsn@sover.net

Nancy Hansen
Canadian Editor
Box 8040
Canmore, Alberta T1W 2T8
e-mail: nhansen@telusplanet.net

CANADA

FALLING ICE—FALL ON ICE, POOR POSITION
Alberta, Banff National Park, Johnson Canyon Upper Falls

On January 19, J. G. was standing at the base of an ice pillar when a climber above dislodged large pieces of ice. One of the pieces hit her and she fell about ten meters down a slope, suffering a compound lower left leg fracture. One person ran out for help. J.G. was evacuated by heli-sling by Warden Service rescue teams.

Analysis

Standing under ice climbers is hazardous, particularly when one is on sloping ground and not tied in to an anchor. Falls on ice with crampons frequently result in lower leg injuries due to the crampons catching while sliding. (Source: Parks Canada Warden Service)

INADEQUATE BELAY—CLIMBER LOWERED TOO QUICKLY
Alberta, Jasper National Park, Malign Canyon

On February 10, at 1600, a Jasper Warden was contacted via cell phone by B.C., who reported his partner had stabbed his right knee with his left crampon while being lowered after top-roping a climb. The Warden Service evacuated B.C. with a wheeled stretcher to the trailhead.

Analysis

His partner lowered the victim too quickly, and as a result, he caught his crampon on the ice causing him to spin and then stab his right knee with his left crampon. Belayers should always pay close attention to their partners while lowering, and the speed should be slow enough so the descending climber can safely negotiate the terrain s/he is being lowered over. Occasionally, a fast lower can result in the belayer completely losing control over the lower, resulting in serious injury or even death. (Source: Jasper National Park Warden Service, L.P.)

FALL ON ICE, INADEQUATE PROTECTION
Alberta, Banff National Park, Louise Falls

On February 14, T.T. was leading the final crux pitch of this popular Grade 4+ ice climb. He placed two or three ice screws above the belay on the steepest part of the pillar, the last one protecting the exit moves onto a low angled section. He began to climb the final steep step, when he fell approximately 30 meters to the bottom of the pillar, bouncing off the low angled section and onto the lower angled terrain below the belay. He sustained an ankle and back injury in the fall. Two mountain guides were guiding clients nearby and lowered the injured climber to the base of the route. The accident was reported by cell phone to Banff Warden Dispatch. Warden Service rescue crews arrived as the injured climber reached the base of the route. He was then evacuated by heli-sling to the valley below.

Analysis

It is sometimes tempting to not place protection after the crux is completed. It is not known why the climber fell, but the distance of his fall may have been significantly reduced had he placed a screw on the low angled terrain between the two steep sections. (Source: Parks Canada Warden Service, L.M., T.T.)

FALL IN CREVASSE—POOR POSITION, INADEQUATE EQUIPMENT
Alberta, Jasper National Park, Athabasca Glacier

On March 16, D.S. and I decided to attempt a ski ascent of North and South Twin, despite the fact that the third member of our party could not come along. The year 2001 was a low snow year, but we felt it was reasonable for the two of us to ascend the heavily crevassed Athabasca Glacier since we had been there several times before without incident. The weather was poor on that early Friday morning, but visibility was sufficient to find a route up the glacier beneath Mount Snowdome. Trail breaking was hard with 30 centimeters of new snow, and the howling wind didn't help as we lugged our 60-pound packs up the glacier.

We reached the serac zone beneath Mount Snowdome at about 1000 hours. On our left was a thick maze of crevasses. On our right were the house-sized blocks of ice from the seracs high above. I chose a line as close to the crevasses as seemed reasonable, and we picked up the pace a bit to get through this dangerous section faster.

I suddenly sensed darkness, a complete loss of orientation, and the horrible realization that I was falling. I saw the bottom coming up to meet me...fast!

After what seemed an eternity, the rope stopped my fall. I slammed against the crevasse wall about five meters above a ledge. My heavy pack was killing me as I pulled myself upright and spent the next minute trying to control my breathing. To say I was freaked would be an understatement.

I took my pack off—not the easiest thing to do given that I had forgotten to put on a chest sling. Taking off the skis turned out to be quite a chore as well. I figured I was about 12 meters from the sunlight above. I was in a slot about 20 meters deep, 12 meters long and two meters wide. Wild ice sculptures at either end and above made me cringe. I could see that the reason I fell so far was because we had been skiing parallel to this crevasse. D.S. told me later he thought for sure he was going to follow me in as the rope zippered into the snow before his eyes. It stopped three meters in front of him.

It didn't take very long for the walls of ice to start sucking heat out of me. While moving uphill, I only had a few layers on to avoid overheating. Dangling in my harness, I couldn't get anything out of my pack. Above, D.S. had by now built an anchor and removed himself from the system. He followed the rope, started digging and knocked loose some of the overhanging ice sculptures. Fist-sized ice cubes came raining down. Why don't we wear helmets when ski mountaineering?! One chunk hit my left thumb, another my left shoulder. It was now impossible for me to climb with the prusiks.

D.S. and I tried communicating, but I could barely hear him and he couldn't hear me at all. Finally he determined to get help. Having only two people on our team made that undertaking less than perfect. I was hoping he wouldn't fall into another crevasse on his way down!

Using the extra coils of rope in my pack, I lowered myself to the "floor" about five meters down. Once there, I put on every bit of clothing I had in my pack. Where I was standing was just over a meter wide, which meant that I wasn't yet near the real bottom. The snow just in front of me turned out to be bottomless when I probed it. I tried to take my mind off the tenuous nature of my stance.

I dug out my crampons and attempted stemming up with one hand on the prusiks. That worked for about five meters, but then the walls bulged outwards, and I could go no further. I resigned myself to waiting and sat on my pack trying to keep warm. I took out my sleeping foam pad and rolled it out over my head as a poor substitute for an icicle umbrella. I spent five hours sitting there contemplating life and death and hoping a serac didn't choose that moment to enter my crevasse.

In the meantime, D.S. had reached one of the Athabasca Icefield tourist buses and called for help. Despite the unstable weather, the rescue helicopter managed to pick up the wardens and bring them to the scene. Within 30 minutes they fulfilled my wish about seeing the light of day. D.S. and I had tied several knots in the rope between us, following the theory that they would slow down a crevasse fall. (They didn't!) The knots proved to be problematic when they were pulling me out. The wardens also tried to retrieve my pack, but because of the weird angles and obstacles, they were unable to bring it up quickly. Since we were very much in the active serac zone, we decided to abandon the pack.

I didn't know it at the time, but I was quite dehydrated and suffering from shock. As the EMS lady coaxed me into the ambulance I kept thinking, "Bah, I'm okay, I don't need to take an ambulance..." It wasn't until I was sitting down in a warm place re-hydrating that I realized just how messed up I was. I was surprised about some of the symptoms of shock. Emotionally I was a mess. I experienced spontaneous uncontrollable crying and the shakes for the duration of the ambulance ride to Jasper.

The next day, we drove back home down along the icefields parkway in beautiful weather. What I found interesting is how my psyche shifted from, "I'm glad to be alive," to "I wonder if I can get my pack out?" All that clarity and simplicity was slipping away. Two weeks later three of us ventured up to the crevasse only to find car-sized chunks of ice and snow covering the whole area.

Analysis

Prevention is better than falling in. Check the snow pack! Probe when in doubt. Consider alternative routes. In our case we ignored the "fresh blowing snow combined with low snow year" clues.

• Pay particular attention to the lay of the land. Sometimes there are exceptions to the direction of the crevasses.

• Practicing crevasse rescue in the gym is great, but it's not the same. It is hard to simulate the real weight and cold and working with gloves, etc.

• Falling in with skis is not the same as falling in with crampons and an ice ax. There is no way to catch yourself as you go in on skis.

• Three people on any glacier are way better than two. On a known heavily crevassed glacier, three people should be considered mandatory.

• Bring a VHS radio and know how to use it. In the winter the margin of error is considerably smaller than on a summer trip.

• Bring walkie-talkies to communicate with the party on the outside.

• Bring a pair of mini ascenders. I am confident that I could have worked these in lieu of the prusiks and my injury. Working 5mm prusiks on a 8mm rope with knots under 250 pounds of tension is no picnic in freezing temperatures! (Source: R.M.)

FALL ON ICE, INATTENTION
Alberta, Banff National Park, Professor Falls

On March 20, after instructing an ice climbing session on this popular Grade 4 ice climb, J.M. tripped on easy terrain while descending to the second rappel. He fell over a six meter pitch and sustained a dislocated shoulder and a back injury. One member of the party walked out for help, and the victim was evacuated by heli-sling shortly thereafter by Warden Service rescue crews. (Source: Parks Canada Warden Service)

Analysis

Care and attention are necessary even on easy ground, especially when one has crampons on. (Source: Nancy Hansen)

RAPPEL ERROR—INADEQUATE ANCHOR, WEATHER, CLIMBING ALONE
Alberta, Jasper National Park, Mount Snowdome, Slipstream

On the afternoon of March 24, M.G. and C.G. made their way up the Dome Glacier to establish a basecamp below Mount Snowdome. Their objective was to climb "Slipstream" (alpine grade VI, water ice grade 4+, 925 meters). This alpine ice climb forms most years on the east face of Mount Snowdome. The party awoke early and discussed plans. The weather was changing for the worse, and M.G. decided not to climb. C.G. decided to solo the route and departed camp at 0400. He took with him one ice screw and a 40-meter section of 8.5mm rope. His intended route down was the standard descent route to the south. At daybreak, M.G. observed his partner ascending the route.

By midday he was just below the top of the route. Throughout the morning the weather had continued to deteriorate with cloud build up and increased winds. At this time M.C. observed his partner starting to rappel the route. He saw a couple of rappels before the clouds descended and C.G. was obscured from view. About 30 minutes later M.C. observed a large avalanche coming out of the cloud and down the route. Fearing that his partner had been caught in the avalanche he quickly made his way back to the road and called for help. His call was patched through to the RCMP. The Jasper Warden Service was notified at 1630. Wardens on scene at 1650 spotted what they believed to be C.G. high on the climb continuing to make his way down.

However, high winds and poor visibility over a distance of five kilometers made it impossible to be absolutely certain that what they were viewing through their spotting scope was C.G. At 1744 the rescue helicopter arrived from Golden and flew to the route with rescuers on board. The body of C.G. was spotted on the glacier at the base of the climb approximately 900 meters below his last observed position at mid-day. At 1825 C.G.'s body was slung off the glacier to the staging area at the Icefield Center where an ambulance was waiting. C.G. was pronounced dead at the staging area.

Analysis

C.G.'s body was found with the climbing rope passed through his belay device, a prusik attached and the ends of the rope tied together. All indications point to anchor failure being the likely cause of his fall. There was no Abalokov cord attached to his rope, which indicates that he may have been using a bollard or icicles to rappel off. He was found with his Abalokov hook, but his only ice screw was not on him when he arrived at the ambulance. C.G. was not found in avalanche debris, so whether the initial avalanche or subsequent unseen avalanches contributed to his fall is unknown. It is likely that C.G. decided to rappel the route due to strong winds and poor visibility on the summit ice cap. The ice cap is crevassed, so navigating to the descent route in poor visibility while climbing alone would have been very hazardous. The avalanche forecast for the day as issued by the Jasper Warden Service rated the avalanche danger in the alpine as high. (Source: Jasper National Park Warden Service, R.W.)

FALL ON SNOW, POOR POSITION
Alberta, Jasper National Park, Parker Ridge

On May 6, a group of mountaineers were practicing crevasse rescue at Parker Ridge. The group was working in roped teams of three. A person on one end of the rope would jump off a corniced ridge, while the other two people on the rope would arrest the fall and then perform the "rescue". A.L.'s group performed the rescue practice once successfully and then changed the order of the rope team to practice again. A.L. was facing away from the cornice when the person on the end of the rope jumped off. A.L. was spun around quickly and ended up with a spiral fracture in her lower leg. The rest of the group splinted her leg and then carried her out on a tarpaulin. (Source: A.L.)

Analysis

This particular accident may have been prevented if A.L. had been facing the direction of the cornice and "victim". It is also possible that the group was getting "aggressive" in their practice, and the victim jumped farther than before, creating a significant sudden jerk on the rope. In a real crevasse fall, team members may not always be facing the right direction, but the rope should be kept tight enough between members to ensure there is no sudden and great force of pull on the rope. It is important even in practice to ensure that the rope is kept tight. (Source: Nancy Hansen)

FALL ON ROCK, POOR CONDITIONS
Alberta, Mount McGillivray, Kahl Crack

On July 16, D.W. was leading the third pitch of this 200 meter high 5.5 rock climb. The crack in which he was supposed to be climbing and placing gear was wet, so he climbed on the rock just beside the well traveled route. A handhold pulled off, and he fell 15-20 meters. Natural Resource Services, Kananaskis Country, was called by a nearby mountain guide. D.W. was suffering from a sore lower back, but declined an ambulance ride. (Source: Ken Wiley)

Analysis

It is possible to view the third pitch from its base. When D.W. and his partner realized the pitch was wet and out of condition, it would have been wise to consider retreat. (Source: Nancy Hansen)

FAILURE TO FOLLOW ROUTE—STRANDED,
Alberta, Banff National Park, Mount Haddo

On July 21, after completing the North Glacier Route on Mounts Haddo and Aberdeen, a party of four began descending the "easy" south face of Mount Haddo as described in a local climbing guidebook. After a couple of rappels and steepening terrain, they became stranded and called Warden Service dispatch with a cell phone. They were evacuated by heli-sling shortly after.

Analysis

The guidebook gives two options for descending from Mounts Haddo and Aberdeen. The option this party chose is described as "easy scrambling from almost anywhere on the Southwest Ridge." In reality, the terrain is at best fifth class and exposed. The easy descent involves climbing up and over Mount Aberdeen. Many parties have experienced epics trying to descend the south face of Mount Haddo. (Source: Parks Canada Warden Service, Editor)

FALL ON ROCK, HANDHOLD BROKE, SOLO HIKING/SCRAMBLING
Alberta, Jasper National Park, Mount Woolley

Late in the afternoon on August 5, D.E. was approaching the col between Mounts Woolley and Cromwell, en route to the Lloyd MacKay—Mount Alberta Hut. D.E. pulled on what appeared to be a solid handhold, but it broke free. D.E. lost his balance and fell backward, tumbling head over heels, over a three meter high rock step, for a total distance of 20 meters. Aside from several cuts and bruises and spraining both hands, D.E. received a severe blow/puncture to his left knee. D.E. was able to get to the Mount Alberta hut by 2200.

On August 14, D.E.'s parents notified the Jasper Warden Service that their son was overdue. D.E. had left a detailed route description of his extensive hiking trip with his parents. The Mount Alberta Hut was the first place checked by a warden in a helicopter. D.E. was found at 1000 hours. Although his knee had been healing without infection, he was unable to fully weight bear on his leg.

Analysis

While this accident does not necessarily fit into the mountaineering category, it is included to indicate the seriousness of solo travel in the mountains. D.E. had planned to do a multi-day hike/scramble in a very remote area with no trail system and extremely few visitors. Had this accident occurred on a different leg of his journey, further away from the hut, the search for him would have been more complex. D.E. was lucky his injuries were not more debilitating, as he would have had no one to care for him or activate rescue services sooner. Fortunately, D.E. left a detailed route plan with his parents and strict instructions for when to call for a rescue if he was not out. (Source: Jasper National Park Warden Service, L.P.)

EXHAUSTION, EXCEEDING ABILITIES
Alberta, Banff National Park, Mount Temple, East Ridge

On August 10, a party of three was reported overdue to Warden Service dispatch. They had been about 30 hours on this alpine grade IV, 5.7 route when they were located at the start of the gullies that lead to the summit icecap. A Warden Service rescue crew was dropped off on the ridge and determined that the climbers were okay but exhausted and requesting evacuation. They were evacuated by heli-sling.

Analysis
The party underestimated the route finding and commitment factor on this moderately difficult alpine route. (Source: Parks Canada Warden Service)

STRANDED, EXCEEDING ABILITIES
Alberta, Banff National Park, Mount Lefroy, Lemire Route

After 32 hours on this alpine grade IV, 5.7 route a party of two was reported overdue to Warden Service dispatch. They were located near the top of a rock buttress below the summit ridge and evacuated by heli-sling at their request.

Analysis
This is a seldom-climbed route with only cursory route information available. The party encountered difficult route finding, poor rock quality, and difficult climbing. On such alpine routes, guidebook gradings cannot always be taken at face value. (Source: Parks Canada Warden Service)

STRANDED, INADEQUATE EQUIPMENT
Alberta, Kananaskis Provincial Park, Mount Sir Douglas

On August 29, two climbers ascended Mount Sir Douglas via the East Ridge, alpine grade III, 5.6. Before beginning the route, they had decided they would descend the same way, instead of taking the longer but easier west ridge descent route. The climbers summited at a late hour, and decided to descend the west ridge after all. They bivouacked at a notch between the ridge and the glacier below and then attempted to descend the glacier the following day. The glacier was bare ice and steep enough to demand crampons, which the climbers did not have. They used their radio to call for a rescue. (Source: Kananaskis Country Alpine Specialists)

Analysis
It is important to minimize one's pack weight when attempting a big alpine route. However, one must not leave any essential items behind. These climbers took a big risk by leaving their crampons at home. (Source: Nancy Hansen)

ROCKFALL
Alberta, Banff National Park, Mount Patterson, East Face

On September 5, a party of three started early for a two-day ascent of this alpine grade IV, 5.6 route. The route involves climbing a few pitches of glacier ice followed by mixed climbing on snow and rock.

Part way up the lower ice tongue, one of climbers decided to turn around while the other two continued. At 2100, the third climber could see that the other two had only gained another 125 to 150 vertical meters and had not yet reached the upper rock face. On the second day the climbers continued. On one of the upper pitches rockfall from above hit one of the climbers, and he sustained a fractured arm. The climbers were able to take shelter in a nearby cave. The uninjured climber continued alone to the summit to summon help.

On the third day the party was reported overdue. A Warden Service rescue team responded and easily located the cave as the climbers had stamped "HELP" in a snow slope nearby. The rescue team was inserted below the cave by heli-sling. The victim was treated and then lowered out to where he could be evacuated by heli-sling. The second climber was found near tree line on his descent. He was flown to the staging area. (Source: Parks Canada Warden Service)

Analysis

Rockfall is a common natural hazard in the Canadian Rockies. Many routes become more dangerous as the day wears on and the sun warms up the mixed snow and rock faces. This party appeared to be moving quite slowly on the route, and their timing may have contributed to the accident. (Editor: Nancy Hansen)

FALL IN CREVASSE, CLIMBING UNROPED, INADEQUATE EQUIPMENT
Alberta, Jasper National Park, Athabasca-Andromeda Glacier

On September 5, P.P. and A.B. departed the climber's parking lot below Mount Athabasca at 0430 to climb Mount Athabasca via the Athabasca-Andromeda col. On reaching the toe of the glacier they roped up and put their crampons on. They had 25 meters of 8mm rope. Much of the lower glacier was clear of snow, and the crevasses could be easily avoided. As the snowcover increased they found travel arduous as their footsteps punched through the poorly consolidated snow surface. Higher up on the glacier they started to walk on rock deposits along the flank of the glacier below Mount Athabasca. Feeling that they were safe from crevasses on the rock, they unroped. Traveling on the rock was awkward with crampons so they moved back onto the glacier and continued unroped. They found the snow more consolidated at this elevation of approximately 2900 meters. A.B. was following P.P.'s track when he stepped through a poorly bridged crevasse and fell 22 meters. The time was approximately 1100. P.P. established voice contact with his partner, who reported that he was on a snow bridge and had hurt his chest. Lowering a rope end to his partner, A.B. tied in. There was insufficient rope-end left at the surface to set up a crevasse rescue system. A.B. was unable to ascend the rope due to his injuries. Putting on extra clothes, A.B. got into his emergency shelter as his partner ran for help. At 1320 the Jasper Warden Service was notified. By 1525 a rescue party of six Park Wardens had been helicoptered in close to the accident site on the glacier. Using a mechanical winch a Warden was lowered to A.B. who was secured to a line at 1605. He was hoisted to the surface without complication by 1620. A.B. was flown to the staging area below Mount Athabasca where he was transported by ambulance to the Jasper hospital. His injuries were cuts and bruises.

Analysis

All the glaciers in the vicinity of the Columbia Icefields are in a rapid state of retreat. This contributes to the highly crevassed character of the glaciers. This party should have roped up once they left the rocky flank of the glacier. They believed they were traveling on ice, but it was in fact consolidated snow. Second, the rope they were using was not long enough to set up a crevasse rescue system. A.B. was very fortunate not to have been injured worse during the fall. He was also fortunate he was not wedged at the bottom of the crevasse or buried by the falling snow bridge. Crevasse bridges at this time of year are often very weak. Recent snowfall had masked signs of sagging snow bridges over crevasses. (Source: Jasper National Park Warden Service, R.W.)

CARDIAC ARREST—FALL ON SNOW
Alberta, Banff National Park, Mount Temple, East Ridge

On September 15, a party of two was ascending the Aemmer Couloir variant of this route. This is a snow and ice gully of 45 to 55 degrees. About halfway up the route one of the climbers started suffering from chest pains and respiratory distress. Shortly after, he fell approximately 150 meters to the bottom of the gully.

His partner descended and detected no vital signs. He continued descending for help. A Warden Service rescue team responded and evacuated the victim. It appears that he suffered a cardiac arrest prior to his fall.

The victim had a history of heart troubles. (Source: Parks Canada Warden Service)

FALL ON ROCK, FOOTHOLD BROKE—FAILURE TO TEST HOLDS
Alberta, Mount John Laurie (Yamnuska)

On September 29, two experienced climbers were ascending the Redshirt route on Yamnuska (II, 5.7). On the fourth pitch, leader I.H. (51) traversed left, clipped a bolt, and then began the five-meter, somewhat diagonal down-climb to the next belay station. He could not see the belay below him, and spent a few minutes searching around. As he stepped back and forth, his foot settled on a patch of loose rock that gave way. He lost his balance and fell upside down in a pendulum fall of five to six meters. His rack of rock protection ended up between his back and the rock, injuring his ribs. He was able to climb back up to his partner and was then lowered to the base of the route. Fearing further injury on the steep hike out, the climbers called Natural Resource Services, Kananaskis Country, when they reached the base of the cliff.

Analysis

Yamnuska is a very popular traditional rock climbing cliff with over 70 multi-pitch routes. It is also renowned for having sections of loose rock. Climbers must be vigilant about testing each and every hand and foot hold before trusting their weight to it. Some climbers argue that it is wise for the lead climber to wear a pack, even if it only has some light clothing in it. Packs have been known to prevent climbers from suffering back injuries during a fall. On the other hand, packs have also been known to cause falls when they catch on rock or pull the climber off balance. (Source: I.H. and Nancy Hansen)

FALL ON ICE, CLIMBING UNROPED
Alberta, Banff National Park, Mount Aberdeen, North Glacier

On October 14, a party of five was climbing the lower tongue of this snow and ice route. The party solo climbed the ice tongue until the angle reached about 45 degrees, and then they stopped to set up a belay. One of the climbers fell, tumbling about 200 meters into talus below the ice. Two of the party members rappelled to him while two others lower on the ice down-climbed. They reached him in about ten minutes, where they joined a mountain guide who had reached G.L. first. G.L. was unconscious but regained partial consciousness after some time. He was in critical condition with head injuries, abdominal trauma, and an ankle fracture. One of the members ran out for help. Another found G.L.'s cell phone and climbed up to a pass to get reception. He was able to reach the Warden Service, saving a significant amount of time for the initiation of the rescue. The patient was evacuated by heli-sling to Lake Louise. He was later transferred to Calgary by air ambulance. The victim survived his injuries.

Analysis

Soloing "easy" ice is common. However, even on low angled ice a slip will result in very rapid acceleration and a potentially long fall. Climbers should consider this risk before deciding to solo climb. It is not known how long it was before the party was able to make cell phone contact to request help, but it likely saved at least one hour. (Source: Parks Canada Warden Service, Sandy Sauer)

FALL ON ICE, INADEQUATE PROTECTION
British Columbia, Lillooet, Oregon Jack

On January 7, H.C., S.P., and I headed into the hills south of Cache Creek for a day of ice climbing on "Oregon Jack."

The ice was in good shape, although quite "platey" on the surface. The angle of the climb was moderate, so H.C. placed only four screws on the pitch, which looked like a reasonable number to us on the ground—although subsequent events were to prove this wrong. Just below the top, he placed his second tool, causing a large plate to fracture around both tools. H.C. fell a long way and came to rest upside down, unconscious, tangled in ropes and gear, and dribbling blood from out of his helmet.

S.P. was dragged out from behind the block where he was sheltering and was whipped over to the base of the route, but did a good job of maintaining control of the rope. Luckily, while the "slack" rope was a tangled mess, the "active" line ran smoothly, and we were just able to lower H.C., who started to regain consciousness within a minute or two, to the ground. The screw that caught him was about 29 meters up, and we were climbing on 60-meter ropes.

S.P., a fireman, assessed H.C. and determined that while H.C. was pretty dazed and banged up, he was basically okay. A climber from Seattle walked out to raise the alarm while we got H.C. out of most of his climbing gear and stretched out comfortably on pads and packs. Half an hour later, it seemed advisable to move him away from the "line-of-fire" at the base of the waterfall, and once he was up it became apparent that he was well enough to be able to move, so we set off toward the hayfield about 400 meters away.

With support from S.P. on one side and me on the other, H.C. hopped, hobbled, and slid his way out in about half an hour. At the hayfield we were greeted by an RCMP officer, a couple firemen, and several medical personnel with an ambulance. Three hours later, after being X-rayed, examined, stitched, glued, and generally cleaned up, H.C. was released.

Analysis

So, lessons? Well, I've only been witness to one other long leader fall on ice, and it came about in much the same way—the fracturing of the surface ice around tool #1 when tool #2 was placed too close to it. Shoulder-width apart is not enough when the ice is brittle. Either stick strictly to diagonal placements, or keep your tools far apart if you must place them at the same height—the width of a door (about 80cm) should be perfectly safe. Think "X," not "H."

Lesson #2: Double ropes are great on ice. Both ropes got notched (probably by tools) and the active line had a partially fused sheath (maybe rope on rope?), but they did their job, and H.C. lived to tell the tale.

Lesson #3: While it is tempting to run it out on moderate ice, it would have been wise to dial in another screw a few meters up onto the finishing pillar. As it was, a screw on the pillar would have greatly shortened H.C.'s fall. Also, having the alternate rope clipped to that piece would have reduced the reliance on the screw that caught H.C. Given the distance between the placements, if that one screw had failed, H.C. would have decked from 40 or 45 meters. Not a pleasant thought...

Lesson #4: People are great when trouble hits, and the natural instinct is to help. The guys from Seattle blew off their day of climbing to raise the alarm and helped to carry packs out. The locals were helpful in shortening the walk out and were ready to help carry H.C., if that had been needed. I had to leave my gear in the route, but a friend from Abbotsford recovered it the next week-end, and I got it back at the Ice Festival. I came out of the whole affair feeling good about my fellow man.

As for H.C., he ended up with a dozen stitches in his scalp, a dozen stitches in a gashed elbow, a few smaller notches glued shut, and a badly wrenched knee. Later, more detailed examination uncovered a small fracture at the top of his left tibia, and he had surgery to screw the chip back in place. A short time on crutches and a while with a cane and he is pretty much okay—a lucky lad! (Source: Don Serl)

CLIMBING ALONE, WEATHER—LOST EQUIPMENT IN STORM
British Columbia, Mount Robson Provincial Park, Mount Robson

During the week of August 27, C.G. set out to attempt a solo climb of Mount

Robson or Resplendent. He made it to the col between the two mountains. During a violent storm his tent was destroyed and ice ax lost. Feeling he no longer had the necessary equipment to continue safely, he activated his personal locator beacon at 1300 on September 3. The signal was received by the Rescue Coordination Center, in Victoria, British Columbia. They notified the Mount Robson Park Rangers who in turn notified the Jasper National Park Warden Service at 1645. The Jasper Warden Service conducted an aerial search for C.G. and found him uninjured at the col at 1922.

Analysis

Mount Robson is a serious undertaking for a party of experienced climbers, let alone a solo climber with minimal climbing experience in the area. It is riddled with numerous hazards ranging from crevasses, to serac fall, to avalanches, to poor weather. A climber must be able to evaluate and select routes to negotiate these hazards. C.G. was warned of these hazards by a Robson Park Ranger before attempting the mountain. If C.G. had not attempted the mountain with other experienced mountaineers, he may have been able to retreat. C.G. was extremely fortunate to have not fallen into a crevasse or to have succumbed to one of the many other hazards of mountain travel. Fortunately, C.G. was carrying a device to activate a rescue, although it did take some time for his location to be pinpointed and then relayed to the appropriate rescue agency. A radio or satellite phone would have allowed him to communicate directly to rescue personnel. (Source: Jasper National Park Warden Service, L.P.)

FALL ON ICE, INATTENTION
British Columbia, Kootenay National Park, Haffner Creek

Haffner Creek is a popular ice climbing area with a number of new mixed climbs. On December 13, a group of mountain guides were doing some training. While ice "bouldering" five feet off the ground, R.O. fell. He landed on his feet on uneven ground, shattering his lower leg in the process. One of the other guides was able to contact the Warden Service by radio. He was evacuated by heli-sling to the highway.

Analysis

Even short falls can have serious consequences, especially when one has crampons on his/her feet. R.O.'s comments were as follows.

"I have been climbing ice extensively for the past eight years and this is the first fall that I have ever taken. The ice I was climbing when I fell was of a very easy grade. I think complacency was the cause of my accident. Stupid accidents like this one are not uncommon among experienced climbers. Climbers need to always be focused and aware, even when the climbing is easy and close to the ground." (Source: Parks Canada Warden Service and R.O.)

LOOSE ROCK
Ontario, Bon Echo, Ottawa Route

On July 21, I.G. was leading the third pitch of the "Ottawa Route" (5.8) at Bon Echo, which rises 100 meters straight up from Lake Mazinaw, when she called out to seconder C.G. that a large granite block had dislodged and was weighing down upon her. Seeing no boaters or swimmers below, C.G. shouted to her to let it fall. As it hurtled past, it gashed I.G.'s leg deeply. She began belaying C.G. upwards but within a minute or so she called down that she was faint from blood loss and shock. She tied off on her pro, and C.G. made his way to her, self-belaying with a prusik cord. C.G., a retired firefighter, treated the gash to stop the bleeding. He then built a full anchor and lowered I.G. a ropelength to the lake. As luck would have it, the park tour boat was passing by and got her to shore. The gash required 14 stitches in hospital.

Analysis

C.G. later remarked that it was fortunate the block did not sever the rope as it came down, which would have made this quick, competent rescue in difficult terrain impossible. Though Bon Echo has a reputation for unstable rock, the regulars noted that last summer saw more rockfall than usual. The weekend before this accident there had been two minor accidents on the heavily traveled route "Fanny Hill," both involving rock breaking off. (Those climbers suffered bruises and minor cuts.) One explanation offered by a geologist was that Bon Echo granite, which undergoes frost fracturing in the winter, was being stressed by the record temperatures experienced during the heat wave of 2001. (Source: David Henderson)

(For the readers' interest, we present the following report from the Yukon Territory's Kluane National Park Reserve on their Icefield and Mountaineering Statistics For 2001. It is interesting to note that there were no serious climbing incidents reported from any of these expeditions.)

During the 2001 climbing season in Kluane National Park Reserve a total of 42 mountaineering expeditions were registered. This accounted for 163 persons spending some 2872 person days in the St. Elias Ranges.

The weather was typically unpredictable. Some expeditions hit it lucky and had few good weather days while others had to wait out long periods of poor weather. Avalanche hazard seemed to be higher this year with many different climbing teams reporting a very weak layer in the snow pack throughout the icefields all season long. Some teams wisely decided to abort or change their planned routes due to the avalanche conditions.

As is the norm, most expeditions were to Mount Logan with only the King Trench and East Ridge routes being attempted. Of the 23 expeditions on Mount Logan this year, 11 were successful to one of the main summits (Main Peak, East Peak, or West Peak). Successful expeditions took from 13 to 24 days to reach a summit, depending on weather and the teams' abilities.

Other mountains that had climbing activity this year included: Queen Mary (six parties); Mt Lucania-Steele (four parties); King Peak (two parties); Kennedy (one party); Walsh (one party); Vancouver (one party); and Pinnacle (one party). The Icefield Discovery Camp was in operation again this season, and its location may be the reason that Mount Queen Mary was a popular destination. Only four of the expeditions were guided. There were also three ski tour expeditions into the St. Elias Ranges in 2001.

Of note was a traverse of Mount Logan up the East Ridge and down the

King Trench by a team from British Columbia. Another B.C. crew did a ski tour of the St. Elias Range from Kluane Lake to Dry Bay, Alaska.

Only one major search and rescue operation occurred in 2001. The incident involved the loss of one of the premiere mountain pilots in the area when his aircraft crashed upon take-off after picking up two climbers in the Mount Kennedy area. The two climbers survived the crash, in which the aircraft ended up 30 meters down a large crevasse.

Other public safety incidents included frostbite, altitude sickness, and other medical emergencies. In each case the climbing party was able to help themselves to their basecamp and fly out. (Source: Rick Staley, Mountaineering Warden, Kluane National Park)

UNITED STATES

HAPE, HACE, AMS
Alaska, Mount McKinley, West Buttress

On May 4, the "Joyful Expedition," led by Chun Byung-Tai, was flown to basecamp on the Southeast Fork of the Kahiltna Glacier by Hudson Air Service. The eight man Korean expedition began their ascent of the West Buttress route on Mount McKinley on the same day and made their first camp at the 7,800-foot level. Continuing up the route the team arrived at the 14,200-foot camp on May 8. On May 9 two members, Kgyoung-Su Han and Chi-Hyeon Pack, began suffering from acute mountain sickness (AMS) with symptoms including nausea, headaches, and lassitude. Accompanied by one healthy teammate, Jinyong Kim, the sick climbers descended to camp one at the 7,800-foot level where they had an extra tent. Later in the day members of the expedition came to the National Park Service camp requesting that we look at Young-Tak Chin (23) who was feeling ill in their tent.

Air National Guard Pararescueman John Loomis and Park Service Volunteer Chris Eng responded immediately and discovered the patient unconscious and not responsive to pain stimulus at 1445. Mr. Chin was sledded to the medical tent where he was put on oxygen and given a shot of dexamethasone. Within ten minutes of being given supplemental oxygen Chin regained consciousness. Nurse practitioner George Rodway evaluated Chin and diagnosed him with both cerebral and pulmonary edema. For the next three nights Mr. Chin remained in the Park Service medical tent breathing supplemental oxygen. Chin's cerebral edema resolved rapidly, but the pulmonary edema remained critical for several days. Each morning and afternoon, when his teammates brought him meals, volunteer Rodway would have him walk around camp without oxygen and then monitor his blood oxygen saturation level. Improvement was slow but steady. The flow rate that Chin was breathing was down to 1 liter/minute on May 11. On the morning of May 12 he was able to maintain his oxygen saturation in the low 80s without supplemental oxygen and the weather had improved.

With the consent of sponsoring physician Dr. Ken Zafren, Chin descended under his own power with supplemental oxygen to the 11,200-foot camp. NPS personnel Joe Reichert, Chris Eng, and Paul Barendregt followed Chin to the lower camp and then released him from NPS care. He descended to basecamp with a teammate, Jeon Woo-song, and they were flown to Talkeetna the same day.

Analysis

The illnesses experienced by two members of this expedition were preventable. Had the Joyful Expedition taken a few more days ascending to the 14,200-foot camp, most likely two members would not have become ill. (The third sick member was later diagnosed with an ulcer and evacuated by helicopter.) Most parties take six to eight days to climb from basecamp to the 14,200-foot level. This group arrived at fourteen on the fifth day climbing. Gaining altitude this quickly does not allow the body enough time to acclimatize and therefore makes one more susceptible to altitude related illness.

HAPE
Alaska, Mount McKinley, West Buttress
At 1245 on May 11, George Payot (63), a member of the Denali French Expedition, approached the NPS 14,200-foot camp complaining of shortness of breath. Payot stated he first began experiencing respiratory problems the previous day when he arrived at the 14,200-foot camp. The Denali French Expedition spent one night each at the 8,000-foot and 9,700-foot camps, three nights at the 11,000-foot camp, and one night at the 14,200-foot camp while ascending the West Buttress. Upon medical examination by NPS volunteer nurse practitioner George Rodway, Payot was diagnosed with mild to moderate High Altitude Pulmonary Edema (HAPE) with audible crackles in his lungs. His O_2 saturation was 64%. He was treated by NPS staff with O_2 at six liters/min via a non-rebreather mask and remained at the NPS camp for further evaluation. By 2050, Payot stabilized with no audible rales at an O_2 saturation rate of 84-86% on two liters of O_2/min. Payot remained on O_2 at the NPS camp for the night of the 11th. By morning, his condition remained stable with clear lung sounds bilaterally. At this time, NPS staff recommended to Payot that he descend. His team agreed to walk him to 11,000-foot camp. However, by 1200 on May 12, he refused any further NPS medical advice or treatment and chose to remain at the 14,200-foot camp while the other members of his team attempted to summit. On May 12, Payot signed a release and left NPS care. He was able to descend without assistance.
Analysis
If the Denali French Expedition had descended to a lower elevation at the initial onset of Payot's respiratory problems, perhaps he would not have needed medical assistance. As with the previous case, note that susceptibility to altitude related illnesses is greatly increased when individuals gain altitude before allowing their bodies to acclimatize properly.

ILLNESS—PREEXISTING CONDITION NOT REPORTED
Alaska, Mount McKinley, West Buttress
On May 14, Chi-Hyeon Pack (27) was evacuated by helicopter from Mount McKinley due to symptoms of a gastrointestinal bleed. A few hours later he underwent surgery for a bleeding ulcer at the Alaska Regional Hospital. (See the May 4 report.)
Analysis
Upon investigation it was discovered that Mr. Pack had a history of GI bleeds. Many of his symptoms were consistent with AMS, so it is understandable that the climbers expected him to recover after rest at lower altitude. Given his prior medical history it was unfortunate that Mr. Pack did not recognize his symptoms for what they were when they did not resolve at lower altitude. The other team members in the Joyful Expedition were willing to evacuate Mr.

Pack, but due to the possible severity of his internal bleeding, it was decided to evacuate him by helicopter.

FALL ON SNOW AND HAPE/HACE—ASCENDING TOO FAST
Alaska, Mount McKinley, West Buttress

At 1430 on May 17, Frainciso Borja (32), a member of the Blue Skies Expedition, was witnessed by NPS Ranger Scott Metcalfe and VIP Kirk Mauthner falling from just below the balcony at 15,200 feet. Borja caught his right crampon on his left pant leg, falling approximately 30 feet where he self-arrested and came to a stop just above Mauthner and Metcalfe. Borja complained of a broken or sprained right ankle. After a patient assessment, it was determined by Bob Mayer, a VIP nurse, that Borja had point tenderness to his left hip also. At 1630, Borja was packaged and lowered to a sled at around 14,300 feet, where Metcalfe with two tail-ropers skied the patient to the 14,200-foot medical camp. By 2000, Borha's condition deteriorated, and he had lost circulation and sensation in his foot.

Concurrently, around 2130 while walking around the 14,200-foot camp, NPS volunteers Moyer and Sherrington came upon an unresponsive climber. Marc Springer (29) of the Vipers Expedition was carried over to the NPS medical tent because of a severe case of high altitude sickness. He was non-ambulatory and barely conscious when he arrived. VIP medical professionals George Rodway and Bob Mayer administered HACE/HAPE related drugs. After only slight improvement to Springer, NPS personnel determined both climbers required additional medical attention and that air evacuation was necessary.

The NPS Lama helicopter flew Borja and Springer, assisted by Ranger Kevin Moore, an EMT, to the 7,200-foot basecamp by 2200. A Pavehawk medical helicopter was waiting at basecamp for them. By 2323, both patients landed at Providence Hospital in Anchorage. Both Borja and Springer spent the night in the hospital under close supervision and were released the next day. Borja was diagnosed with a bruised left hip and severely sprained right ankle. Springer had signs and symptoms of both HACE and HAPE.

Analysis

Borja did a great job using his ice ax to self-arrest. It was a textbook arrest! His pants were very baggy and loose fitting. Had he and his partner been roped up the fall might have been prevented. He was fortunate that a highly trained NPS team was on the spot with proper personnel and equipment.

Springer, on the other hand, simply ascended too fast. He went from 7,200 feet at basecamp to 14,200 feet in four days! It is common to take many more. He seemed pressured to keep up with his partners who were acclimatizing on the West Buttress in order to climb the Cassin Ridge.

FROSTBITE—DEHYDRATION AND INADEQUATE CLOTHING, POOR PHYSICAL CONDITION
Alaska, Mount McKinley, West Buttress

About 2100 on May 18, climbers at the 14,200-foot camp witnessed Ron Morrow (51) take a fall on the fixed lines around 16,000 feet. Morrow made it back to the 14,200-foot basecamp by 2300 cold and tired. His partner Michael Rodriguez reported that Morrow was so exhausted that he fell asleep until around 0700 the next morning. On the morning of May 19 Rodriguez helped Morrow to the NPS medical tent where it was determined by NPS personnel George Rodway and nurse Bob Mayer that Morrow had mild frostbite on his left little finger and full thickness frostbite on the four largest toes of his right foot. Since the foot of Morrow had thawed partially overnight, Rodway and Mayer helped to thaw his foot completely with a warm water lavage. After his foot was thawed, he was unable to walk. Typically an injury of this nature would not warrant immediate transport, but weather forecasts indicated a significant decline until May 24. At 0942 on May 20, Ranger Metcalfe spoke with acting South District Ranger Daryl Miller and other NPS personnel who decided it would be best to do a resupply of essential needs like propane for the 14,200-foot camp and most important, to get Ron Morrow off the mountain. About 1100 on May 20, the NPS Lama helicopter flew Morrow to the 7,200-foot basecamp where he was then flown to Talkeetna via a fixed wing provided by Doug Geeting Aviation. In Talkeetna Morrow took a taxi to Anchorage where he was treated by a frostbite specialist.

Analysis

Upon further investigation, it was determined that Morrow had not enough water to drink, nor had he eaten enough. He got his gloves wet digging his cache at 16,200 feet. Morrow admitted he showed up out of shape and said he was guilty of trying to keep up with a 28 year old! In addition, the weather was poor, he had no overboots and had a history of frostbite 23 years ago in the same foot.

FALL ON SNOW—CARRYING TOO MUCH
Alaska, Mount McKinley, West Buttress

On May 23 around 0800, Priska Landolt (30) of the Glaronia-Swiss Expedition was descending below the fixed lines around 15,000 feet when she hooked her left ski tip and heard a pop in her left knee. She packed the knee with snow and continued to descend with the three other members of her expedition. Around 1000 Landolt arrived at the NPS medical tent at 14,200 feet. Dr. Christian Bannwest, an orthopedic surgeon from Switzerland, assisted her to the tent where he, with VIP medical professionals Dan Cosgrove and Bob Mayer, examined her. Dr. Bannwest determined that Landolt had suffered a tear of her medial collateral ligament and/or her anterior cruciate ligament. Medical personnel considered an evacuation necessary because of the instability and inflammation in her knee.

Cloudy weather and a low-pressure system delayed an air evacuation until May 26. On May 26 at 2000 the NPS Lama helicopter landed at 14,200 camp to fly Landolt to the 7,200 basecamp. At basecamp Landolt was flown to Talkeetna by air taxi. In Talkeetna she stayed the night at the Swiss Alaska Inn, then departed for Anchorage and eventually Switzerland the next day on May 27. A letter of thanks to all involved was received by Ranger Metcalfe on

June 20. Landolt wrote that she had a complete tear of her anterior cruciate ligament.

Analysis

Landolt's expedition was doing a traverse from Wonder Lake on the Muldrow Glacier up and over Denali Pass. After waiting out weather near Denali Pass in hopes of a summit bid, they descended the fixed lines with heavy packs and two sleds. Landolt might have chosen to cache some weight at some point in order to decrease the risk of injury. The expedition had decided to descend to the 14,200-foot ranger camp in order to rest and wait for another summit day.

AMS, HAPE
Alaska, Mount McKinley, West Buttress

On May 26, Mark Hall (42), a client of Mountain Trip, was brought to the Ranger Camp at 14,200 feet complaining of a severe headache and persistent cough. He was treated for Acute Mountain Sickness (AMS) and High Altitude Pulmonary Edema (HAPE) and a possible respiratory infection. After being reevaluated on the morning of May 27th he was evacuated from the mountain via Lama helicopter to basecamp where he was transferred to Life Guard and taken to Providence Hospital.

Analysis

The rate of ascent over the course of the expedition remained within reasonable limits for proper acclimatization at 1000 feet per day. However, on Denali's West Buttress the large jumps in elevation that are generally undertaken within a single day to reach the established camps result in some individuals reacting adversely. The fact that Hall was already experiencing symptoms at 11,200 feet and yet he continued to ascend, and further, that his symptoms continued to worsen on that ascent to the point where he was no longer self-sufficient and still continued up to the 14,200-foot camp rather than descend, are cause for concern. The well-established prescription to descend at the onset of AMS symptoms or at least cease ascent until such symptoms resolve was not followed. And while the needs of the individual must be weighed against those of the group and it is often difficult to make a decision that adequately accommodates both, the decision to continue to 14,200 feet may have hampered this expedition's ability to remain self-sufficient and execute a self-evacuation.

FOOTHOLD GAVE WAY—FALL ON SNOW, PLACED NO PROTECTION
Alaska, Mount Hunter, Southwest Ridge

On May 26 at 1700, James Raitt (27), James Bonnie (27), Mark Paterson, Darren Swift, Richard Cantrill, and Peter Pollard flew to the Southeast Fork of the Kahiltna Glacier to attempt Mount Hunter's Southwest Ridge and the Sultana Ridge on Mount Foraker. Taking into consideration the current snow conditions and recent weather patterns the team decided to attempt Mount Hunter first. At 1900 the team departed Basecamp for the Southwest Ridge of Mount Hunter and camped at the base of the West Ridge.

On May 27 the team moved their camp to the Thunder Glacier at the base of the Southwest Ridge, arriving at 1400. On May 28 the team took a rest day and wanded the route to the base of the Southwest Ridge. On the morning of May 29 at 0400 the team departed camp arriving at the base of the couloir at 0500. The group was traveling in rope teams of two, with Raitt and Bonney being the lead team. Around 0600 Raitt and Bonney had reached a bend in the couloir. They were moving well and saw no need for running protection up to that point. Bonney later stated, that since the terrain was starting to get steeper, he had considered putting in some protection at this point, but continued without it. Moments later a piece of ice on which Bonney was standing gave way. Bonney fell pulling Raitt off with him. Neither was able to self-arrest and the two fell to the bottom of the couloir, coming to rest on the debris cone just above the Thunder Glacier, a distance of approximately 700 feet. The other four members of the team witnessed the fall and descended to render assistance. The two injured climbers were within three meters of each other when the other members arrived.

Raitt sustained injuries to his pelvis and lower left leg. Bonney sustained injuries to his right ankle and ribs and abrasions and contusions to his left hand and forehead. Both patients remained conscious throughout the fall. After Raitt and Bonney were stabilized, Pollard and Cantrill left for Basecamp at the Southeast Fork of the Kahiltna, while Swift and Paterson remained with the injured climbers. While en-route to basecamp, Pollard and Cantrill contacted Talkeetna Air Taxi Pilot Rico Olmstead by CB radio and informed him of the accident. The party was unable to hear Olmstead's response, so Olmstead used air to ground signals to acknowledge receipt of their transmission. Olmstead landed at basecamp and reported the transmission to Ranger Mik Shain. On his own initiative, Olmstead, with climber Mark Westman aboard, flew to the scene to try and gather more information about the accident. Olmstead and Westman were unable to communicate with the two climbers who were en-route to basecamp, nor the climbers at the scene of the accident, but were able to confirm the location and number of climbers involved.

Ranger Mik Shain contacted the Talkeetna Ranger Station at 1050 to inform them of the accident. Initial reports speculated that the accident was caused by avalanche and that there were up to four patients. The Incident Commander, Ranger Joe Reichert, with the Air Operations Chief, Dave Kreutzer, decided to send the NPS contract helicopter to the scene.

At 1221, the Lama, piloted by Jim Hood, was launched with Rangers Gordy Kito and Kevin Moore aboard. At 1223 Jay Hudson launched in a Cessna 206 to provide communication and visual support. At 1254, the Lama arrived on scene. Through hand signals the rangers determined that there were two patients to be evacuated from the scene. Because of the exposure to objective dangers at the accident site, it was decided that Ranger Moore would be short-hauled to the scene. The Lama landed, and a staging area was established at the team's camp on the Thunder glacier. Ranger Moore was short-hauled to the scene at 1313 with a "screamer suit," "Bauman bag," and a backboard. Bonney was loaded into the "screamer suit" and transported to the staging area at 1321 hours, while Moore, Swift, and Paterson put Raitt onto the backboard and into the "Bauman bag."

Raitt and Moore were lifted from the scene at 1334 hours and transported to the staging area. Both patients were assessed at the staging area by Kito and transferred to Air National Guard Pararescue personnel for transport to Anchorage.

Analysis

Raitt and Bonney were both skilled mountaineers having collectively climbed in the French and Swiss Alps, Peru, and Nepal. The objective the team had chosen seemed well within their abilities, and they paid close attention to previous weather patterns, snowfall and route conditions. The team had planned plenty of time for the expedition and was climbing on an appropriate schedule.

As they started climbing the couloir at the base of the route, they made a decision to continue climbing without running protection while being roped together. Bonney stated that at the time of the accident he was starting to consider placing running protection. Unfortunately Bonney's stance gave way before he placed any protection. The injuries that resulted from the fall may have been worse had both climbers not been wearing their helmets.

The severity of many accidents in the Alaska Range may have been reduced by the use of running protection while climbing simultaneously and roped together. Climbing roped on steep terrain, without protection either natural or through the use of pickets and ice screws, always carries the risk of increasing the number of injuries or fatalities while offering little in the way of safety.

There have been numerous accidents on this route despite John Waterman's claim in his book *High Alaska* that this is the "safest... route up Mount Hunter." Two of the four members in the first ascent party were caught in a wet-snow slide while descending this couloir and carried 500 feet to the bottom. Though the first ascent party suffered minor injuries, a team of four experienced climbers, despite placing running protection, fell 1,700 feet down the couloir, which resulted in the death of two of the members.

FALLING ICE, POOR POSITION
Alaska, Mount McKinley, Cassin Ridge

At 2105 on June 16, Jason Kraus (30), a member of the Cold and Stinky Expedition, requested evacuation from the base of the Cassin Ridge on Denali. Kraus had sustained an injury to his left leg from falling ice while belaying his partner, Michael Morris, in the Japanese Couloir. Both members rappelled approximately 500 feet down the couloir where they established a landing zone at the 11,300-foot level for the NPS Lama helicopter. Kraus was unable to walk, yet remained in stable condition until Denali Park Ranger Dave Kreutzer arrived on scene with Lama pilot Jim Hood. At 2247, Kraus was transported to 7200-foot camp where he received primary medical assistance by climbing ranger Karen Hilton and NPS volunteer Sara Ennega. Kraus' chief complaint was point tenderness in his upper left thigh resulting in an inability to bear weight. Lifeguard helicopter arrived at 7200-foot camp at approximately 2300 and transported Kraus to Providence Medical Center where he was treated for a bruised thigh.

Analysis

Proper assessment of the fall line within a couloir can reduce the risk of injury to a climber. Kraus may have been able to avoid injury from ice fall had he and his partner chosen a belay stance out of the fall line of climbers above.

(Editor's Note: All the reports from Denali National Park were edited by Daryl Miller, South District Chief Ranger. The reports he worked from were written by Rangers Roger Robinson, Kevin Moore, and others.)

FALL ON ROCK, INADEQUATE PROTECTION, NO HARD HAT
Arkansas, Sam's Throne

On March 10, a climber (36) was looking at a climb from the top of a route, but he was not tied in. He fell 50 to 60 feet and suffered major head injuries, fractures, and other trauma. He was assisted by other climbers, who transported him via backboard to a helicopter called to the scene. (Source: Anonymous)

Analysis

Each year there are at least a few reports of this kind of accident—both on rock and ice cliffs. The first order of business one should attend to for these top rope situations is setting up an anchor. Hard hats are a good idea for people at the bottom of the cliff or while climbing—to do the job they are made for, which is to protect one's head from falling rocks or objects. In this particular case, a hard hat would not have done much good. (Source: Jed Williamson)

FALL ON ROCK, INADEQUATE PROTECTION, CLIMBING UNROPED, NO HARD HAT
Arizona, Oak Creek Overlook, Griffo

On September 28, a rock-climbing teacher died after falling more than 60 feet from a route called Griffo (5.6) at the Oak Creek Overlook on Highway 89A South of Flagstaff.

According to the Highlands Fire Department, Glennon Wessellman (34), of Cottonwood, sustained massive injuries in the fall, which happened just before 11:00 a.m. Rescue crews hiked to him, and it took about 20 minutes to get Wessellman moved to an awaiting Department of Public Safety helicopter because of the terrain. He was then flown to Flagstaff Medical Center, where he was pronounced dead.

Sgt. Randy Service of the Coconino County Sheriff's Office said Wessellman was a teacher at a Cottonwood charter school. At the time of his fall, he was instructing five students, ages 15 to 19, on how to rock climb.

He was setting an anchor into the rock wall when he lost his balance and fell, Service said. He was not wearing a helmet or a safety rope at the time of the fall. (Source: *Arizona Daily Sun, September 29, 2001*)

FALL ON ROCK, INADEQUATE BELAY ANCHOR
Arizona, Superior, Queen Creek

I was climbing in Atlantis, Queen Creek, on a 5.10, which really has no belay spot directly below the climb, so my belayer set up on the other side of the creek bed, about seven meters away from the wall I was to climb on. All was well until I fell above the fourth bolt. I anticipated the fall, and conveyed this to my belayer. ("Oh shit, I'm falling!!") It probably only took about a second and a half for the fall, but I saw each bolt go by, and I saw three go by and wondered, "Why haven't I stopped by now?" After I did finally stop, I was only about four feet above a ledge, and my belayer was nowhere to be seen. After shouting out, I discovered that she had been pulled off her boulder (not anchored) and swung across the creek bed and slammed into the cliff on the climb's side. As she was using a Black Diamond ATC and not a GriGri, I can't believe she didn't let go of the rope to break her fall. Thank God she didn't, because I would now be toast.

Analysis
What I learned: No matter how much your belayer weighs, anchor them down! I hope someone learns from our mistake and can avoid an accident (of this kind). (Source: Keri Means—33)

ROCKSLIDE
California, Mount Shasta, Avalanche Gulch
On May 21, while ascending the Avalanche Gulch route, a large rock slide occurred, hitting a party of one guide and four clients. Two clients were injured.

The Sierra Wilderness Seminar (SWS) guided groups began their climb early to lessen their exposure to rock fall, which is usually more active in the afternoon. There were several SWS parties on the route simultaneously. One party was at 11,500 feet at 0745 when the rock slide started. As rocks and ice chunks fell, they attempted to move out of the way, but the rocks were moving fast and had enough momentum to cross the gulch where the party was located. Two of the five member team were struck by rocks. Gabriel Artalejo (27) was hit on the forehead, impacting his helmet. He tumbled down the hill 250 feet, lost consciousness, and slid another 250 feet before coming to a stop. The SWS guide descended immediately to Artalejo and did a primary and secondary assessment.

Other SWS guides were notified as well as Search and Rescue. The other guides were able to keep their clients in a safe place while they descended to assist. They made a barricade of backpacks and gear above Artalejo to protect him from continuing rock and ice fall. Artalejo's neck and head were immobilized, and the laceration on his forehead was bandaged.

Another climber, not with SWS, was also impacted by rock fall to the arm, and walked to Lake Helen where he was evacuated by helicopter at 0945.

Patrick Daley (30) was hit on the upper back and on the lower arm/hand. Daley descended with a guide to Lake Helen (10,400 feet), where he was evacuated by helicopter at 1030.

Search and Rescue climbed up to Artalejo and arrived at 1230 bringing rescue gear. Artalejo was back-boarded, placed in a SKED, and lowered to an LZ at 10,600 feet where he was evacuated by helicopter at 1330.

The California Highway Patrol helicopter evacuated all injured climbers and transported them to Mercy Medical Center, Mount Shasta. Both Daley and Artalejo were released by 1600.

Analysis

The snowpack on Mount Shasta was around 70 percent of normal and very warm spring conditions caused a rapid melting. Rock fall usually becomes more prevalent in July and August as the Avalanche Gulch route is surrounded on three sides by higher terrain of loose rocks. This route is notorious for rockfall as the snow melts, and early season and early morning climbs are *usually* safer.

Although climbing helmets are not designed for front or side impacts, this helmet probably made a huge difference in the extent of Artalejo's head injury.

Wilderness rescues often take several hours to days to complete. In this case, the party had to wait six hours in a very exposed and dangerous area before they were evacuated. (Source: Eric White, Matt Hill—USFS Climbing Rangers, Michael Massari—SWS)

FALLING ROCK—CRUSHED HAND
California, Yosemite Valley, El Capitan, Sea of Dreams

My name is Robert. I am a 24 year old Austrian. On April 12, I started soloing the Sea of Dreams on El Capitan. The climbing was excellent—demanding but not dangerous. The hauling was very hard and the nights were uncomfortable due to runoff from melting snow on the summit, but I had full storm gear so it was okay.

On the fifth day, at 3:30 pm, I was halfway through pitch 14, called "Don't skate, mate." I put a sling over a rounded horn and top-stepped in my etrier to place a nut straight up in a crack below a small roof/block-like feature. It is shown as "expanding" in the *SuperTopos* guidebook. I tested the nut, and it was okay.

However, I had to go slightly sideways, which might pull the nut out and then the sling off the horn. This would expose me to a long fall, so I placed a small cam (the size of a blue TCU) and climbed back down in my aiders to test it. I held onto the horn in case the cam popped (it was not sitting perfectly) so that I would not fall onto my daisy sling. I gave the cam a hard bounce, and suddenly there was a loud noise and I saw the small roof (a block of backpack size) breaking off.

The block fell slightly to my left. I know I should have jumped to the right in order to get my hands away from the horn, but things were happening too fast. As a reflex, I held on to the horn and the block hit my left hand. Still standing in my aiders, I realized the injury was severe. The left ring finger was smashed—it was bleeding quite heavily, there was no feeling in it, and it was attached to the hand only by some pieces of skin. The middle finger was injured too, and the whole hand was useless. Luckily, there was very little pain (the nerves were cut off).

I decided to make my way down the wall as fast as possible and to leave all of my gear up there. In the first moments, I did not know if I would be able to rescue myself. Rappelling one-handed is not easy, and I might suddenly feel very weak or do something stupid because I was injured. Also it might be too late in the day for a self-rescue or even a rescue by YOSAR, so I shouted for help. Only climbers on Zenyatta Mondatta shouted back, but luckily the self-rescue worked out well. There were fixed lines on the Sea of Dreams from Big Sur Ledge (top of pitch 14) all the way to the ground, with backup ropes rigged along side them; the ropes were in good condition although they looked like they had been hanging up there for more than a century.

I managed to reach the fixed ropes by means of a small pendulum at the "expanding anchor" (top of pitch 13) shown on the Super-Topo. I rapped down, holding the injured hand above my head in order to diminish the bleeding. Passing knots in the ropes and doing traversing rappels was quite difficult with one hand. I tried to be extremely careful not to lose any critical gear. As I went down "full speed ahead" the GriGri got burning hot and smelled bad; this made me go more slowly and safely. I began checking everything twice, and at one point I discovered that I had clipped in the GriGri the wrong way. Double checking during an emergency is extremely important because, in all the hurry and pain, one tends to cut down on security checks and concentration. Although it's hard to tell—and it would have been much more difficult—I think I might have done a self-rescue without the fixed ropes.

I reached the ground about two hours after the accident. Unfortunately nobody was at the base who might have helped me, so I ran down to the road at El Cap Meadows. Three tourists drove me to the Yosemite Medical Clinic, and I guess I ruined the seat of their car with my blood.

I was flown to a major hospital in Modesto. This caused some discussion because the injury was not life-threatening, and normally the helicopter only flies in such cases. But there are certain time limits within which an injury like this one can be treated correctly, and the doctors decided that the finger might be saved if I was flown out. In Modesto the doctors found that the bones in the finger were broken heavily. The circulation and nerves were cut off as well. There was no way to save the finger. It had to be amputated at the first joint (this means two-thirds are gone).

It took several months of treatment until I could use the hand again, but I never saw this accident as something that changed my life in a bad way. I feel as happy as before, even though it is harder to climb with only nine fingers, I climb better than ever. The accident did not stop me from climbing big walls either—I came back to Yosemite later and soloed Zenyatta Mondatta and other routes.

Analysis

I had been climbing for ten years, including several dozen North Walls in the Alps and previous big walls in Yosemite. I had led many pitches on aid, up to NW A4 or harder. I am as careful as possible and I test every non-bomber placement, and until this accident I had taken only one short fall on aid. Was it bad judgment or did bad luck just finally catch up to me? I don't know. Loose rock and flakes can be avoided for the most part, but sometimes one can not check how loose the rock is. For example, the crack on Sea of Dreams did not expand or make any noise when I tested the nut just before I placed the cam. The block itself looked quite solid—at least a lot more solid than some other stuff I have seen while climbing. Risk, luck, and bad luck are pretty close together in climbing even if one is experienced. (Source: Robert Steiner)

NPS comments: This really was Robert's lucky day. If that backpack-sized block had bounced slightly to the right and hit his head, his helmet would have offered little or no protection. Regarding his effort to signal for help: people on the valley floor can usually hear climbers yelling (especially in good weather), flashing lights at night will usually get a response, and more and more climbers are carrying cell phones or family-band radios as a backup. But none of these options are guaranteed, so the ability and confidence to retreat on your own, injuries permitting, is the final line of defense. A cheater stick and a bolt kit may also be critical to a quick, safe descent. I'd put my money on Robert to get down on his own, but too many El Cap parties these days have neither the experience nor gear. (Source: John Dill, SAR Ranger, Yosemite National Park.)

PROTECTION CAME OUT—FALL ON ROCK, PLACED INADEQUATE PROTECTION, DARKNESS
California, Yosemite Valley, The Nose

On May 14, Brian Smudz and Yanchun Su climbed from the ground to Dolt Tower, without fixing any part of the route. They had planned on one relaxed day on the climb, and they took it on the 15th because of the long first day. They climbed to El Cap Tower and fixed to Boot Flake, but otherwise spent the day relaxing.

Smudz and Su found the climbing straight forward, and Brian freed to 5.11b. The ascent was fairly relaxed, and there were no problems between the two of them. They never had to wait for other parties and weren't pressured by parties below. They saw only two parties in all: one group passed them at El Cap Tower on Tues. and rapidly climbed out of sight. Another group was below them, but they either retreated or climbed more slowly than Smudz and Su, because they never caught up and weren't seen again.

On May 16, they climbed to Camp Four and bivvied there. On May 17, they climbed to Camp Five, fixed no pitches, and bivvied there. On May 18, they arrived at Camp Six at about 1300 and Brian started up the next pitch. About halfway up a thunderstorm moved through the Valley, with lightning near Sentinel. They got rain and hail, and a small waterfall formed above them. Brian retreated to Camp Six for an hour until the storm passed.

They had to decide whether to stay at Camp Six that night or push for the top. Earlier they had figured they'd stay there if they arrived late and were tired. There were no important psychological factors at work. They wanted to summit but would also be willing to bivvy there. By this time it was about 6:00 p.m. and they would be climbing most of it in the dark, but they decided to go on anyway. They had headlamps and had climbed in the dark in the past.

It took Brian about 20 minutes to jug back up to his high point, and by that time it was dark. The rain had mostly evaporated, and they continued by headlamp with no problems.

After a couple of more leads, with Yan belaying about 100 feet below, Brian reached the Alcove. He had put in a fair amount of protection below the Alcove so he was running low on quickdraws. Although there were belay bolts in the back of the Alcove, they were out of position to be worth using for protection so he climbed past them, leaving his last piece of protection, a cam, two or three feet below the start of the Alcove.

The Alcove itself is a triangular hole a few feet high, with the apex at the bottom and one side of the triangle forming the roof. The low angle floor is only 4th class. The left wall sticks out forming a right facing corner. The route follows a crack that arches out to the right at the top of the hole. The climbing as you exit the Alcove is 5.9.

Brian clipped his rope with a quickdraw to a fixed piton a few feet beyond the Alcove. He moved out another five to eight feet, still on 5.9 slab with fingers in the crack. Here he was able to place a bomb-proof nut in a vertical crack and clip through it with another quickdraw. About two feet further was a fixed #1 or #2 stopper, placed straight up under the flake forming the crack. He clipped a quickdraw to it and yanked hard to the left, right, and down, but the stopper was solid so he clipped in his rope. He had some distance to go to the belay and was low on quickdraws, so he reached back and removed the previous piece.

The climbing was harder now, maybe 5.10d, still feet on slab and fingers in an under-cling with one or two fingers. It was probably harder in the dark, since small holds might not be as easily detected. He was getting a bit tired but was still comfortable.

While standing below the fixed stopper, he reached out to the right about five feet and found an under-cling pocket in the crack big enough for one or two fingers. He decided to use the pocket for protection. He placed a #2 or #3 Metolious Tri Cam straight up in the pocket, added a quickdraw, and tested it as he had the previous pieces, by yanking down hard, twice.

Because the hold was now blocked, the moves were now harder, 5.10, and as he was wearing his wall boots, he decided to go on aid. He clipped his daisy to an etrier and clipped the etrier to the TCU. He gradually weighted the etrier with his right foot. He was confident in the placement, but would wait until he was fully on the TCU before clipping in his rope.

Just as his weight came fully on the TCU, he heard it shift and saw the cams open a bit, but he had no time to react. In less than a second it popped. His next protection was the fixed stopper, only five feet to the left, but it also ripped out, landing literally in his lap. Having cleaned the next nut, he was left with a 15-foot swing pivoting on the fixed pin, roughly ten feet lower and ten feet to the left. This would sent him directly into the right facing wall on the far side of the alcove.

As he was falling he had rotated 90 degrees to the left, and he swung with his left foot tucked behind him and his right out in front in the direction of the swing. He wasn't conscious of the swing, and he hadn't selected the position of his limbs.

His right leg took the impact on the wall directly on the bottom of the foot. There was no slide, bounce, or crumpling that might have lessened the impact. He looked down and saw that his foot was angled out to the side and already noticeably swollen, but he still didn't think that he'd received anything more than a sprain, at the worst. He called to Yan that he'd taken a bad fall. She had felt almost nothing and thought he'd only been pulling slack.

Brian was pissed, and full of adrenalin. He hauled himself back up to the piton, free climbed further. He replaced the nut he had cleaned. Climbing 5.10 on one leg he moved up and right several feet to the TCU slot and replaced it. This time he rammed it in hard, so deep he could now get his fingers in also. He yanked on it and it seemed good so he continued face climbing—on one leg—to the belay bolts. (The belay is in the middle of the 33rd pitch per the Reid topo. They were out of synch because he had not stopped to belay at the Alcove but had climbed through it.)

He hauled the bag by pushing out—body hauling—on one leg. After Yan came up he led the 5.10b crack on aid—no real problem although it took a long time—and continued up the bolt ladder to the bolts at the lip. It was starting to get light by now. He couldn't do the 5.7 face section to the summit belay tree, so Yan led that. They topped out at 0700.

Since the fall, there was little pain as long as his foot did not touch the rock or anything else. He was wearing high-top wall boots and he kept the right one on his foot as support. He realized that he'd be unable to hike or crawl to the Valley by any route including the East Ledges descent. They were supposed to meet a friend in the Valley on Saturday. He contacted him via one of the family band radios they all carried and asked him to call the NPS. He hoped he could hobble with support up the slope to the helicopter LZ.

His foot was still fairly pain free until an air splint was put on it. Then it began to hurt. He describes it as though his leg were over open flame or hot charcoal—so bad that he didn't want to do anything. It took 25 mg of morphine to get the pain down to where he could make it to the summit without being carried.

Analysis

Yan was belaying with a GriGri, clipped to her harness, and a 60-meter x 10.5-mm rope. She was about 100 feet below, but out of sight. There was no appreciable rope drag as Brian led.

He thinks that, because it was dark, he wasn't thinking about a swinging fall. He could see the corner but didn't realize the full danger of that kind of impact. (Actually, the impact and injury could happen by falling vertically onto a ledge. It could have been worse.)

He back-cleaned the other nut to get the quick draw, because he felt he was running out of them and didn't want to disassemble the quickdraws on his cams. He also had longer runners over his shoulder but didn't want to take the time to rig them as quickdraws. He simply trusted the fixed nut. He now wonders if the crack holding the fixed stopper was in fact expanding. Brian usually doesn't use nuts in horizontal cracks and doesn't clip into fixed nuts. Re the TCU, he thinks he simply should have jammed it deeper the first time.

Brian Smudz has been climbing for ten years, leads GriGri free to 5.10b comfortably, also harder, aid A4. He's climbed several short aid routes in the east. He had climbed no complete walls in Yosemite but had climbed partway up the Nose twice previously, once with his brother and once to Dolt Tower with Yanchun Su, his partner this May. He is a Wilderness First Responder.

Yanchun Su has been climbing for four or five years, but with little leading. She has led GriGri free 5.9, aid A2.

On this ascent Brian led almost all the pitches and did all hauling (because Yan weighs only 100 pounds and couldn't haul the bag.) Yan led a few easier pitches. For storm gear they had synthetic bags, Bibler bivy sacks, and rain suits.

As for injuries, he experienced a pilon fracture of the right foot (medial malleolus fracture), and the tibia was split up the shaft one-third of the way to the knee. It required surgery, with internal fixation (internal hardware). Ten months later there is still some pain, and he is not running yet. (Source: John Dill, NPS Ranger, Yosemite National Park)

FAULTY USE OF CRAMPONS—FALL ON SNOW
California, Mount Shasta, Wintun Ice Fall

On June 24, David Lowe (24) was glissading at 13,500 feet with his crampons on. His crampons caught and threw him into a tumble, and his leashed ice ax penetrated his thigh from hip to knee. He fell approximately 2000 feet.

David Lowe and his party had climbed the Hotlum-Wintun route on the northeast side of the mountain. Lowe, and many in his party, had very little climbing experience. Although this route is not technically difficult, it does have steep sections and crosses above hazardous areas on the Wintun Glacier. On their descent, he decided to glissade wearing his crampons and his ice ax leashed to his wrist. About 13,500 feet on a 40-45-degree slope, the heels of his crampons caught, tumbling him into an out of control fall. He came to rest at about 11,500 feet, where the slope had decreased to about 30 degrees. This area was right above a cliff over the Wintun Ice Fall.

His party summoned help from a commercially guided Sierra Wilderness Seminars trip. Two guides, Miller and Rodriguez, responded and used their cell phone to contact search and rescue around 1430. They assessed and stabilized Lowe's injuries. He had abrasions all over his upper body, and his ice ax had entered his thigh just below his pelvis and exited near his knee. It was deep in his leg and their concerns were that he had ruptured his femoral artery.

USFS Climbing Ranger, Harrington, who was at 10,400 feet on the south side of the mountain, was contacted and responded through whiteout conditions. He arrived at the scene at 1630 and found the injuries to be stable and bleeding under control. Lowe showed no signs of shock. They continued to monitor his condition waiting for air transport. A volunteer from Siskiyou County Search and Rescue arrived at the scene at 1900, and they wrapped Lowe in sleeping bags to maintain his body temperature. At 2030, a California Department of Forestry Bell Super 205 short-hauled Lowe in a litter with an attendant. He was taken to a lower elevation where he was transferred to the

California Highway Patrol helicopter and then transported to Mercy Medical Center, Mount Shasta. Luckily, the ice ax had done little damage internally.

Analysis

The USFS Climbing Rangers and the retail shops that rent mountaineering equipment for Mount Shasta work hard every season to educate climbers about the use of ice axes and crampons. Unfortunately, every year there are accidents on Mount Shasta from improper use of equipment, even after people have been informed. Glissading with crampons can be hazardous to your health! Usually, leg fractures occur from this type of accident, but amazingly, Lowe had no fractures.

An added note is that cloudy conditions and the time of day made this rescue difficult. (Source: Eric White, Matt Hill—USFS Climbing Rangers, and Michael Massari—SWS)

PROTECTION PULLED OUT—FALL ON ROCK
California, Yosemite Valley, Middle Cathedral Rock

On July 12th at 1:00 p.m., a fisherman in Yosemite Valley reported seeing two climbers fall from high on Middle Cathedral Rock. After speaking with this witness, I hiked up to the base of the wall, where I found the bodies of Myra Eldridge of Boulder, CO, and Thomas Dunwiddie (ages unknown) of Denver, CO, just east of the Direct North Buttress route.

No one else witnessed the accident. Its exact cause will never be known, but certain things are clear from the condition of the climbers' equipment at the time they were found.

The team was leading with two 9mm ropes, and both climbers were properly tied to both ropes. Dunwiddie was equipped as leader, with each of his two ropes passing through Eldridges's belay device (an ATC). About 25 feet of each lead rope separated the two climbers; no lead protection was found on either rope.

Their anchor—which appears to have pulled in its entirety during the accident—consisted of the following. One ⅜-inch Alien and one #4 Black Diamond Stopper were clove-hitched together to one of the lead ropes approximately three feet from Eldridge's tie-in point. Two double-stem Camalots, .5 and .75, were each independently clove-hitched about a foot and a half apart on the other lead rope with 15 inches separating the lower piece from Eldridge's tie-in point. There was no evidence that bolts or other fixed protection were involved in the anchor.

All of the anchor pieces were severely damaged, though it is impossible to know whether that damage occurred when they were pulled out or during the fall and final impact. Nevertheless, the two Camalots were each bent in a similar way suggestive of a severe downward force after being placed in a vertical crack.

A loose quick-draw and a few carabiners were also found at the base. Their original purpose could not be determined, and they may have simply unclipped from the falling climbers—a common occurrence.

Analysis

Both Dunwiddie and Eldridge were skilled climbers, and in the days prior to their deaths they had completed a number of challenging free and aid routes in the Valley. Based on the location of the bodies, and on a topo of the Direct North Buttress found in their possession, they were probably on the DNB at the time of their accident. Rated at 5.10c and known for both its length and route finding difficulty, the DNB includes several sections of "run out" climbing and loose rock.

What can we learn? This accident hits close to home for most climbers because the party involved was very experienced with difficult climbing and familiar with Valley rock—as have been at least a third of Yosemite fatalities, historically. Other factors, such as rock fall from above, may have been involved, but the prime suspects are basic anchor and leading concepts that all of us are often tempted to ignore: avoiding anchors in suspect rock, sharing the load to an adequate degree, and stuffing in that first (and second) lead piece right off the belay. If you can't meet these criteria, continue on with the realization that your survival may depend only on your climbing skill and on the quality of the next handhold. At least five other cases of complete anchor failure (protection pulling out—not breaking) have occurred in the Park in the last 30 years. (Source: Lincoln Else, Climbing Ranger, Yosemite National Park)

AMS—ASCENDING TOO FAST, LATE START, EXCEEDING ABILITIES
California, Mount Shasta, Avalanche Gulch

On July 16, Jans Hogenacker (22) and his party of seven—who had little experience and were unable to recognize the symptoms of AMS as they developed—were climbing the Avalanche Gulch route on Mount Shasta and stopped at 13,200 feet at the base of Misery Hill. Hogenacker appeared sick, could not walk, and had difficulty breathing. As often happens, their late ascent left them in cloud-cover, with some electricity in the air.

Siskiyou County SAR was notified at 1433 and at 1730, the California Department of Forestry Bell Super 205 flew three SAR team members to Sargents Ridge at 11,200 feet. It was too cloudy to fly any higher. The three SAR members were planning on climbing Sargents ridge to Misery Hill. (This is a slightly technical and exposed climb.) At 1950 a brief clearing allowed the California National Guard CH-47 helicopter to lift the SAR members to 13,200 feet at the base of Misery Hill. Another climber informed them that Hogenacker and his party had descended on their own when they believed he wouldn't be rescued. They were spotted from the air at 12,400 feet in an inaccessible area. The rescue was aborted.

On their descent, Hogenacker improved and was able to walk out on his own.

Analysis

The group members' inexperience presented them with several problems. Climbing late in the day and into severe weather limited rescue capabilities. Also, not recognizing the signs and symptoms of AMS put their whole party at risk. The biggest problem was involving SAR team members in risky rescue attempts when no one in Hogenacker's party was able to resolve their situation without help. (Source: Eric White, Matt Hill—USFS Climbing Rangers)

FALLING ROCK
California, Mount Shasta, Avalanche Gulch

On July 18, Scott Eisenbarth (25), a guide for Shasta Mountain Guides (SMG), was descending with two clients on the Avalanche Gulch route at 1015 when he was struck on the side of the head by a falling rock. They were at 11,800 feet, and he was aware of the rockfall, having asked the clients to move out of its fall line when he was hit. As he lay unconscious, one of the clients used his radio to call other SMG guides who were at a higher elevation.

The other guides responded and notified Siskiyou County Search and Rescue. As the guides arrived, they did a primary and secondary survey, stabilized and monitored Eisenbarth. Another SMG guide from the West Face route assisted in bringing gear from the USFS rescue cache at 10,400 feet. Eisenbarth was stabilized in the SKED (litter) and lowered 1,000 feet on snow, then carried to an LZ at Lake Helen.

With a clearing of cloud cover at 1415, Siskiyou County Search and Rescue flew in the California Department of Forestry super 205 helicopter to Lake Helen and transported Eisenbarth to Mercy Medical Center, Mount Shasta. He was later transferred to Mercy Medical Center, in Redding, where he was treated for head trauma and a skull fracture. Fortunately, a full recovery was expected.

Analysis

Avalanche Gulch is one of the least technical and most popular routes on the mountain, but it also has the highest exposure to rock fall.

Eisenbarth was wearing a helmet, and although he had a side impact around ear level, injuries probably would have been worse without it.
(Source: Eric White, Matt Hill—USFS Climbing Rangers)

FALL ON ROCK, INEXPERIENCE
California, Yosemite National Park, Daff Dome

On September 15 at 1520, Anne Venturelli (33) had top-roped about 30 feet of a 5.7 climb known as "Western Front" on Daff Dome. Venturelli was unable to complete the pitch and was attempting to tension traverse across the face to get in line with the top anchor so she could be lowered. She slipped and spun across the face, striking her head and back against a ledge. She was wearing a helmet but received a laceration in the basal skull area. She lost consciousness and came to rest on a ledge.

By the time two companions had climbed to her, she had regained consciousness. Another companion went to the road and reported the incident to a 911 dispatcher.

Park rangers responded to the scene by 1530. Rangers ascended to her and provided patient care while a ten-person rescue team was assembled to conduct a litter lowering, which was accomplished by 1743. She was then transported by wheeled litter and, after reaching Tioga Road, was transferred to an ambulance. (Source: Maura Longden, SAR Ranger.)

Analysis

In an interview with Jeff Schimon (27), one of her companions, he indicated that Ms. Venturelli did not have much outdoor climbing experience. He offered that if she had had more experience outdoors, including falling, she might have fared better. He also indicated that she has not been climbing since. "Her husband won't let her. He won't climb if she doesn't. They're both in it together." (Source: John Dill, NPS Ranger, Yosemite National Park)

FALL ON ROCK, PROTECTION, INEXPERIENCE, INADEQUATE FOOD
California, Yosemite Valley, El Capitan, Mescalito

On September 24, on the sixth day out, Caroline Brugvin (24) took a lead fall on the 20th pitch of the Mescalito rock climbing route on El Capitan. She fell 40-50 feet, colliding with the rock multiple times. As she received several minor injuries and a painful injury to her left shoulder, Brugvin was unable to continue the climb, so her partners, David Jonglez (25) and Jeremie Ponson (22), signaled for a rescue. Visitors alerted the NPS at 1930 that evening.

Earlier in the climb, they all shared leads. Caroline made it sound like they swapped leads in a pattern, but later David said that it was not preset who would lead what. Usually whoever cleaned the last pitch would lead the next pitch.

Friday the 21st they spent five hours struggling with a portaledge they had borrowed from the French Alpine Club. It had been put together backwards, so they had to rebuild it on the wall. They ate normally on Friday evening but really didn't eat much because they had spent so much time dealing with the portaledge.

On the evening of the 22nd, they discovered that they had left one of their two bags of food back at Camp Four. David said it was about two thirds of their food. This didn't really concern them, and they didn't see it as a reason to retreat. Caroline said, "You can work two days like that [without food] and a lot of people don't have a lot of food." David later said that it is common for them not to carry much food on a wall. They had food bars for breakfast at about 400 calories each. They also had 12 slices of bread and a fair amount of rice salad. Caroline estimated that they had one-and-a-half days of food per person left at normal consumption when they discovered the shortage. This left them no cushion if they were delayed, so they planned to ration what they had. They also had a bag of caramels. They had brought 40-45 liters of water, which proved to be plenty.

After discovering the food shortage, they decided they needed to climb faster than the four pitches per day they had managed, so on Sunday the 23rd they started trying to do five pitches a day. Caroline said that they didn't consider retreating, since they thought it was impossible.

Caroline said she was leading as fast as the others but was very slow cleaning. She didn't know how or didn't have the strength to clean the pitons and some of the boys (especially David) were mad it took so long. She said Jeremy was never mad. "David got mad but it wasn't his fault, it was his way of being.

He puts pressure for everyone to be perfect." They did have some arguments, and these started from the 21st, before the food shortage added pressure on them.

She also had to spend a lot of energy hauling since she's so light. She weighs about 50 kg. They carried two haul bags and a double and a single portaledge. They would lead with a five-ml tag line and pull up the haul line at the top of the pitch. The haul line was 100 meters or more, allowing them to haul one bag, then the other, on the same long line.

Caroline cleaned pitch 19, and David was frustrated because she had to leave some pins behind and was slow in cleaning. But since she had cleaned, it was her turn to lead pitch 20. David said he was happy that she wanted to lead it. She said she didn't look at the topo before the pitch. She had maybe looked at it the night before, but she had no idea of the difficulty of the pitch. It was just her turn to lead.

Pitch 20 is mostly aid. It ascends a right-facing corner which turns into a traverse to the right, past a bolt, then ascends another crack straight up to a second bolt. Using this bolt as a pendulum point, the leader swings five meters to the right, then climbs a short distance to a cluster of bolts. These bolts are considered a false, or alternate, belay, since the pitch continues, finishing up a right-facing, right-curving corner to the belay ledge. Rope drag can be a problem because of the traverses and the pendulum.

Caroline wanted to avoid rope drag, and she also needed all the gear, so she cleaned a lot of Friends early in the pitch. At the first bolt (per Super-Topo) she hauled up her free-climbing shoes and free-climbed four to five meters. At the pendulum bolt there were slings and 'biners. At this point she did not notice exceptional rope drag. She pendulumed over about five meters, which was fine. Then she climbed to the three-bolt false belay. She cleaned all her protection after the pendulum, in order to avoid rope drag that would be caused by the zig-zag path of the rope, although she stated that she was getting scared about the fall potential at this point.

She wanted to stop at this belay and called down, "I'm at the belay," but her friends said, "No, no, continue [to the actual belay]." She also wanted to clip her rope to these bolts as protection, but her friends told her not to, that it would be too much rope drag. She thought that it would be okay with a long sling, but she had no slings with her, just lots of protection hardware. She was afraid to call down for a long sling because at this point they were trying to hurry, and because of the pressure she'd felt from David. She spent about five minutes at the false belay bolts.

She was very afraid at this point, because she thought that if she fell here she would die. She considered clipping the bolts for protection and removing it later, but she isn't sure why she didn't do this. Instead, she continued up, with her last protection the pendulum bolt. She found the C1 crack after this to be "special." (Later she said it was expanding.) The rock was not good and the crack narrow and shallow.

She put in one piece, a 0.2 DMM cam, and clipped the rope to it temporarily, but knew the piece would probably only hold her body-weight, not a fall. She moved up on aid and placed a second small DMM cam, which she knew was also not very good. (She later said that she was not sure if she had this second piece. If the second piece was there, she must have clipped it to the rope, because she did not leave or lose anything in the fall.) She had an aider on this piece. Her habit was to climb with one aider for each foot, without a sub-aider. The aiders were free, not clipped to daisies.

The third piece was a #.5 Camalot (purple). She remembers feeling relieved that this seemed to be good enough for a fall. She clipped an aider to it and weighted with her right foot. As she shifted her weight, perhaps to lean down and unclip the aider from the last piece, the Camalot pulled out and she fell. She remembers feeling a momentary tug, as one of the lower pieces resisted and then failed, but she did not notice any resistance from the other lower piece. She remembers falling upside-down and seeing the Merced River. Jeremie, her belayer, said there was not a lot of slack in the line. He saw her falling sideways. He belayed with a GriGri and didn't feel much force during the arrest. She remembers hitting everywhere—head, back, shoulder etc. She also remembers screaming, but said she doesn't usually scream when she falls.

After falling vertically, the pendulum bolt took over, swinging her to the left. She hit three times on the swing and finally stopped at almost the same height as the belay and just a bit to the right. She estimates the fall as approximately 45-50 feet vertically.

When she hit the end of the rope she "collapsed" or lost consciousness and was leaning over backwards. They yelled at her, but she just wanted to be left in peace. She felt it was an emotional collapse, fainting, and not a physical loss of consciousness from injury. In fact she could hear and understand what people were saying to her but didn't care. This has occurred to her before, though not when rock climbing. They yelled at her to get her to clip the tag line into her power point, which she did. Then they hauled her over to the belay ledge.

Her left shoulder hurt, but she thought it was just a cam sticking into her because the gear was all over her. David said he could see right away that her shoulder was lower and the shoulder blade was sticking out. She didn't feel well and collapsed again, and David slapped her to get her to respond. She knew right away, though, that she was not seriously injured.

She wanted to stay and thought maybe she could still jumar out or that they should just climb and leave her on the ledge. But she finally realized that she couldn't even sit up. David said he knew that they would need to find assistance as a first plan, so they started yelling for help immediately.

Caroline said she checked her watch at the pendulum and it was 3:00 p.m. Her estimate is that the fall occurred around 3:30 p.m. David thought the accident occurred between 4:30 and 4:45 p.m. and they were yelling for help around 5:00 p.m.

They yelled the words "help" and "SOS." There was no response from climbers on the wall and no response from people they could see along the road below. A group on the bridge at El Cap Crossover stopped when they yelled and they shouted, but it was unclear if it was in response to their cries. They yelled from 5:00 p.m. to dark (about two hours) and they continued to signal after dark with headlamps and camera flash.

A rescue was effected in the morning, after communications that night.

Analysis

Mescalito was their first climb after arriving in Yosemite, since they wanted to start "strongly." Mescalito is rated VI 5.8 A3 and is a 26-pitch climb on very steep rock.

Caroline Brugvin, from Switzerland, had two years climbing experience, leads 5.11a/b trad and A2+. Prior to Mescalito, she had aid-climbed only three single-pitch practice climbs in "school." She thought the aid climbing on Mescalito was easier in terms of the actual pitches but the climbing was longer. It was her first time in Yosemite and her first big wall. She had never done hauling before and knew nothing at all about it. She had climbed on granite before, in Chamonix. She had climbed with David since Spring 2001 as a friend, not as a client. She had not climbed with Jeremie before.

David Jonglez had been climbing for 10-12 years and leads 5.11b trad, A3-4. He had lots of aid experience. He climbed in Yosemite in 1994 (Nose, Half Dome) and 1996 (PO, Zodiac, Salathe). He works as a mountain guide at home. He has also climbed in Greenland, Peru etc. David was the boss on Mescalito. He and Jeremie had climbed together before.

This was was Jeremie's first time in Yosemite. He has only climbed in France. He felt the climbing here was less technical than at home. He felt it was easier to read the routes here. (Donna Sisson, Lincoln Else, John Dill—Rangers, Yosemite National Park)

(Editor's Note: There were a few other accidents in Yosemite that do not appear in the narratives. These include four "rappel failure/error" situations on Royal Arches. In each case, the climbers became stranded, usually after dark, because either they were off route or did not understand how to use their equipment. One team rappelled to a point where, after they had shouted for help, the rangers instructed them, "You can walk down from there.")

FAILURE TO FOLLOW ROUTE, CLIMBING ALONE, EXPOSURE, INAD-EQUATE EQUIPMENT/CLOTHING, WEATHER, INEXPERIENCE
California, Mount Shasta, Avalanche Gulch

Henry Clardy (41) was planning on climbing the Avalanche Gulch route on the south side of the mountain, starting on September 24. Clardy had little mountaineering experience but had attempted Mount Shasta in August. On that climb he did not summit due, apparently, to AMS. He had returned by himself in September.

Without checking the weather forecast or the current climbing conditions provided by the U.S. Forest Service, he began his climb from Horse Camp (7880 feet) at 0700 on the 24th. A storm was forecast for that afternoon and evening and during the day many signs of its approach were visible. Thinking his illness during his August climb was from too much food, he brought only a bag of trail-mix and a Camelback water pack. He wore cotton jeans, a long sleeve cotton t-shirt, a light insulated windbreaker, mid-weight boots, thin leather gloves, and a felt hat.

He did not notice the approaching storm, and when he summited around 1500, the storm began. Clardy removed his rimed (icy) glasses and unknowingly wandered off-route from the summit plateau (13,800 feet) into the steep Mud Creek drainage on the southeast side of the mountain. In the whiteout on the steep scree slopes, he fell and tumbled several times.

The storm dropped between six inches to over a foot of new snow with the snow level around 9000 feet. He realized he was lost and kept himself awake all night huddled by some rocks during the storm. He was attracted to the lights from the town of McCloud 6000 feet below and miles south. He continued at first light and, around 7000 feet, climbed out of the Mud Creek Canyon into the forest. He crossed a prominent logging road but continued past it toward McCloud. He spent his second night in a ravine against a log—around 5000 feet. The morning of the 26th, he decided to go back to the road and follow it.

The Horse Camp caretaker noticed the empty tent on September 24 and notified the USFS Climbing Rangers and Siskiyou County SAR. On 9/25 the search began with rangers following the route to 10,400 feet and the California Highway Patrol helicopter searching from the air. The helicopter was limited by winds and cloudy conditions. On the 26th, two rangers climbed toward the summit while two other rangers and Siskiyou County SAR searched the southeast side of the mountain from above 5000 feet. Clardy was found at 5000 feet, seven miles southeast of his original trailhead, at 0930 on the 26th. The ranger performed a full assessment and found mild signs and symptoms of hypothermia, bruising, abrasions, and possible superficial frostbite on Clardy's fingers, toes, and face. He was taken to Mercy Medical Center in Mount Shasta, where he was treated and released.

Analysis

Although this incident is not uncommon, it reminds us of the preventative actions we should take before a climb, even in California. Changes in weather can happen any time of the year on Mount Shasta. Climbing conditions are usually poor in September due to rockfall. It has snowed on Mount Shasta even during the peak of summer, and the average summer high temperature on the summit is below freezing. There is also a fine line between going light and being prepared. Avoiding cotton and carrying the "ten essentials" is always recommended, and we encourage climbers to wear a helmet. (Source: Eric White, Matt Hill—USFS Climbing Rangers)

(Editor's Note: The above report of a hiker-turned-climber is included for it's educational value for all.)

FALL ON SNOW—UNABLE TO SELF-ARREST, CLIMBING ALONE AND UNROPED, INADEQUATE EQUIPMENT
California, Mount Shasta, Sargents Ridge

The Mount Shasta area had a late winter start with very dry conditions on the mountain. The ridge routes, which are popular at this time of the year, were in poor shape, with loose rock and icy patches.

At approximately 1300 on December 29, a solo climber on the Sargents Ridge route came across a climber who had fallen from approximately 12,500 feet on Sargents Ridge to 11,900 feet in Avalanche Gulch. The injured climber, Tom Malzbender (41), had separated from his partner and was alone at the time of the fall. Due to the rocky conditions, he was not wearing crampons and had tried to traverse an icy area where he slipped and tumbled down into Avalanche Gulch. He came to a stop on a 36 degree scree slope. The climber who spotted Malzbender assessed and stabilized him, finding that he had sustained multiple rib fractures, an ankle fracture, a punctured lung, and major facial lacerations. After bandaging Malzbender, he went for help and contacted Siskiyou County Search and Rescue at 1405.

The California Highway Patrol helicopter flew to 11,500 feet, where rescuers then climbed to Malzbender. They were able to stabilize him and load him into a litter. He was hoisted and transported to Mercy Medical Center.

Analysis

Party separation is a common problem on Mount Shasta. Malzbender's partner was too far ahead and was unaware of his fall. Malzbender was unable to recognize that the rock he was walking on was covered with a layer of ice and a dusting of snow on top. He was not wearing crampons or a helmet. (Source: Eric White, Matt Hill—USFS Climbing Rangers)

(Editor's Note: Go to www.avalanche.org or www.mtshastanews.com or call 530-926-9613 for current climbing conditions, avalanche advisories, and weather forecasts in the Mount Shasta Wilderness.

As for other California reports, there were four incident reports received from Joshua Tree National Park this year—not counting hikers and "scramblers" who became stranded or fell. The climbing accidents were three falls on rock—two of which resulted in fractures—and one rappel error that resulted in rope-burned hands.)

FALL ON ICE, INADEQUATE PROTECTION, MISCOMMUNICATION
Colorado, Ouray Ice Park

In January, a 140-foot fall at the Ouray Ice Park resulted in fatality for an experienced climber, Pete Ro, who was participating in a master's ice climbing class with a group who had extensive experience ice climbing. He had just led up a pillar of ice. When he reached the top he yelled what sounded like, "Off belay," or "Okay." But he was not clipped into the top-out anchors. One of the nearby guides heard him yell this out. The man yelled out, "Off belay!" again, but was still not clipped in. Hearing the command, his belayer went off belay, so when Mr. Ro leaned backward or lost his balance, he fell off, hitting a ledge on the way down." (Source: Taken from a report by Marc Beverly PA-S)

(Editor's Note: This case has more details to it, but is currently in potential litigation. Ouray Ice Park is a busy place during the festival. Communications can be difficult. Climbers, whether they are experienced, relatively new to the sport, or clients of a guide, need to follow basic and obvious directions, such as voice commands and clipping in to anchors.)

FALLS ON ROCK
Colorado, Black Canyon of the Gunnison National Park, Cruise Route

On June 17th, Zach Alberts (20) fell while leading a climb of the 5.10+ Cruise

Route. Alberts was climbing about ten feet above his last piece of protection when he lost his footing, slipped, and fell, sustaining possible fractures to both ankles. Alberts' climbing partner contacted North Rim ranger Ed Delmolino at 9:30 p.m. Delmolino treated Alberts' injuries and monitored his condition through the night until rescue operations could begin the following morning. Park and local rescue teams raised Alberts up the North Chasm wall over 1,500 feet to the rim of the canyon. The mission took about five hours and over 25 rescuers to complete.

On July 9th, Martha Moses (41) fell while lead-climbing Cruise Gully after she and her partner abandoned a climb on the Leisure Route. Moses was climbing 50 feet above her first protection in intermittent rain when she apparently lost her footing, falling and tumbling about 80 feet and sustaining severe head injuries. Her partner contacted ranger Ed Delmolino, who responded along with a paramedic from a local EMS squad. The nighttime litter evacuation involved lowering her down the remainder of the gully in rain, lightning, and continuous rock falls.

Moses was then raised over 1,500 feet up the North Chasm wall to the rim and flown by helicopter to St. Mary's Hospital in Grand Junction, where she underwent surgery for a skull fracture.

The entire operation took 12 hours and involved 50 rescuers and support personnel, including a number of local, county, and volunteer rescue squads. These two operations constitute the most significant technical raises to date in the park. (Source: Linda Alick)

(Editor's Note: We have had very few reports from Black Canyon of the Gunnison over the years.)

FALL ON ROCK, INADEQUATE PROTECTION
Colorado, Eldorado Canyon, Bestowal Crack

My son Chris (17), our friend Eric (17), and I traveled to Eldorado Canyon for guided climbing July 5th. After completing Bestowal Crack, we were in the process of walking off the backside and down the talus slope adjacent to the west face of the Bestowal, when, at 0930, we witnessed and were first responders to a 25-foot ground-fall, resulting in injuries and subsequent evacuation by ambulance.

As I recall, our guide Duncan Burke and I, had descended about half way down the talus slope with the boys following about 30 feet behind us. I think we were midway between the "Out To Lunge," and "Hair City" routes, as we passed a climber and belayer on the west face of the Bestowal. A quick glance at them left me thinking, "How asinine is that," because [there he was] 25 feet up, either setting a piece of pro or clipping into a piece, with one piece clipped about ten feet below him and an arc in the rope nearly reaching the ground, then going to the belayer standing on top of a five-foot boulder ten to 15 feet from the face being climbed.

As I looked back down to pick my footing I remember a flash of movement on the edge of my peripheral vision snapped me back to see the fallen climber on the bounce or just as he hit. He appeared nearly horizontal and about two feet off the ground at that instant.

We scrambled over to find him dazed, lying on his back on a hump of ground and rock. The rope ran loosely from him up to the first piece of pro about 15 feet up, and then down, still in a pronounced arc, to the belayer on the boulder above where he landed. The belayer stood looking down and fairly calmly said, "Bummer, man," but seemed pretty dazed by what he had witnessed and apparently was unable to render assistance at that time.

The boys ran down to the ranger hut at the entrance to the park to summon help. Duncan and I remained with the climber to prevent him from moving and packed our ropes under either side of his torso to take some of the weight off his back, which was lying directly on a ridge of rock.

After about 15 to 20 minutes, a ranger or park employee arrived, said he had EMT training, called in a request on his radio for an ambulance, and began assessment of the climber. By this time both ankles had swollen considerably, but on removal of his shoes, he could move all his toes.

As more assistance arrived, we left to continue our climbing. It appeared to taken a considerable length of time before the climber was finally loaded into an ambulance; my guess is around two-and-a-half hours, in spite of his being approximately 100 to 150 feet from the road, and as I remember, there was some sort of dispute over jurisdiction between different ambulances that arrived. (Source: Randy Roberts—50)

FALL ON ICE, INADEQUATE EQUIPMENT, INADEQUATE PROTECTION
Colorado, Rocky Mountain National Park, Longs Peak, East Face

On August 3 at 0700, Jeff Snyder (24) was leading over the icy Mills Glacier to the base of Stetner's Ledges III (AI 1 5.8) on the East Face of Longs Peak. Snyder had planned to fix anchors in rock at the base of Stetner's Ledges and then belay Joe Verela, Jr. and Joseph Verela, Sr. (ages unknown) across the ice. Snyder was using the party's only ice ax and was wearing winter driveway gripper-type cleats over his shoes in place of crampons. Snyder was 60 feet out on the AI 1 ice without protection and only 10 feet away from rock protection possibilities when he lost his footing and began sliding. Snyder slid approximately 35 feet before self-arresting. He lacerated his right knee on sharp rock protruding from the ice. Snyder then dropped the ice ax to Joe Verela, Jr. so that Verela could get to him and help. However, before Verela could get to Snyder, Snyder lost his position and slid the remaining distance to the rocks. Verala bandaged Snyder's knee and went for help. Rocky Mountain National Park rescuers responded and evacuated Snyder by litter and Flight For Life medical helicopter to Fort Collins, CO. Snyder underwent one hour of surgery and received 30 staples to repair the 10-inch long laceration.

Analysis

In this case, shortcuts led to long lacerations. It is a common yet sometimes dangerous practice among alpinists to skimp on equipment in order to cut back on weight. The Snyder party had only one ax and no real crampons among three persons. Modern ice axes are very lightweight, and there are many models of crampons to chose from that will work on a hiking boot in this sort of terrain. Also, the leader did not protect this section, which might have helped to offset the lack of proper crampons. One method of placing protection here, yet saving on weight, would have been to cut bollards into the ice and sling them. It was an easy section of ice, yet slippery and dangerous, as is the nature of ice.

Snyder did execute a proper self arrest, which minimized his injuries. Unfortunately, when he gave up the team's only ice ax to his partner, he was unable to hold his position. (Source: Jim Detterline, Mark Magnuson, Mark Ronca—Rangers, Rocky Mountain National Park)

TRANSIENT ISCHEMIC ATTACK (TIA)
Colorado, Rocky Mountain National Park, Glacier Gorge

At 12:15 pm on August 5, I (43) suffered a transient ischemic attack (TIA) four pitches up The Barb on Spearhead.

As I belayed Kelli's (my climbing partner) lead of the fourth pitch I began to have strange sensations in my left leg. The small stance I was standing on was cramped, and I tried to shake things off without success. Gradually, over a period of about 15 minutes (and as Kelli completed the 40-meter pitch and arrived at the next belay) I lost the ability to weight the leg, and noticed my left hand going numb. As she put me on belay, I yelled up that I was having some troubles but would try to climb anyway. I cleaned the belay anchor and attempted to climb but could not move. At this point we decided to retreat. There was only one other party on the face, high on Syke's Sickle, so our efforts would have to be unaided. I reset the anchors, and after a brief discussion we decided Kelli would down-climb the upper part of the pitch (runout face climbing, by the way) to within the 30-meter mark of the rope and set an anchor to lower off of and clean the pitch. By the time she reached me at the belay I was losing the ability to speak and could no longer keep my body positioned upright. However I did not suffer any loss of consciousness or mental function.

Below us were a series of overhangs that would make a plumb line rappel retreat to the ground impossible with a single 60-meter rope. We were about 25 meters above Middle Earth, a variable ledge system that crosses the entire face. I suggested the best way off would be to traverse Middle Earth to the route Syke's Sickle where I knew rap anchors were. We set anchors and rappelled to the ledge (I was able to use my right hand to brake and just let the left side of my body bump and slide against the wall), and then Kelli led across the ledge system, placing gear where necessary so I could pull on it as I dragged myself to follow. We found anchors on Syke's Sickle and after two more rappels were on the ground.

Kelli ran to some fellow climbers packing up to leave, and one of them began to run out to the trailhead for help while his partners came to my aid. Through a series of fantastic coincidences, Geoff Friefeld, a doctor friend of mine (albeit a breast cancer specialist) was at Black Lake and had a brand new set of walkie-talkies. His party started back to the trailhead as he immediately ran up to lend us assistance. Through a series of radio relays, word reached the trailhead within 45 minutes, and a helicopter (already on its way up from Denver to assist a broken ankle victim on Longs Peak) was diverted to me. Geoff and one of the climbers assisted me down the talus to a small cairn where the helicopter could land. By the time it reached me my symptoms had mostly resolved. I was in the emergency room at Boulder Community Hospital by 6:00 p.m.

Analysis

This was an unexpected major medical emergency in a relatively remote location, and therefore it is difficult to suggest preventive measures. A 10:00 a.m. start for this route is certainly later than recommended, but we felt confident we could complete the climb in a few hours. It was very fortunate that I did not lose consciousness during the incident. Once we decided we were capable of a self-rescue (indeed we had few options), the fact that we had only a single 60-meter rope significantly changed our options for retreat. Our self-rescue was aided by a thorough knowledge of the rock wall we were climbing on. It was critical knowing the location of the overhangs below that barred a straightforward retreat, the location of anchors on the neighboring route Syke's Sickle, and the high/low points of the talus cone below the wall. It was also important that we were both able to keep our cool and think clearly throughout a very scary situation.

I thank Kelli for helping to save my life. I have fully recovered and, some medical concerns aside, am now back to my old climbing ways. (Source: Steve Levin)

FALL ON ICE, CLIMBING UNROPED, INADEQUATE EQUIPMENT
Colorado, Rocky Mountain National Park, Longs Peak

On August 8 at 0745, Scott McLeod (23) and Dana Drummond (age unknown) were ascending the North Chimney (II AI 1 5.6) on the East Face of Longs Peak. Although primarily a rock route, the North Chimney contained hard alpine "black ice" at its base and as patches inside the chimney. They were ascending unroped in order to get a faster approach to the Diamond Face. McLeod slipped on ice and fell 70 feet down the North Chimney. McLeod landed on both feet but sustained closed injuries to his left ankle and right heel, as well as minor abrasions to legs and arms. McLeod rappelled the remainder of the distance down North Chimney with the assistance of other climbers. Rocky Mountain National Park rescuers met McLeod at the base of the chimney, splinted his injuries, and transported McLeod to a landing zone area on Mills Glacier. Flight For Life medical helicopter picked up the patient and transported him to St. Anthony's Central Hospital in Denver, CO.

Analysis

The North Chimney Route is frequently used as an approach to highly technical pure rock climbs on the Diamond Face of Longs Peak. However, the North Chimney may be considerably more dangerous than the Diamond routes due to poor quality rock, loose rock, frequent rockfall, black ice, occasional large icicles falling out of the D1 exit chimney from the top of the Diamond, and multiple parties climbing on loose rock. There have been an increasing number of accidents on this route in recent years. The North Chimney Route should be taken seriously by climbers. When and where to rope up is a personal decision that each climber makes. In this case, a roped belay in a chimney known for poor rock, frequent rockfall, black ice, etc. would have been a good choice. Climbers should also have full situational awareness when climbing this route as to climber activity above and below them, and to the many objective hazards of the route. The benefit of wearing crampons when crossing ice or climbing mixed terrain is evident. There are many lightweight models of crampons now available that fit hiking boots and do not take up much space.

McLeod, his partner, and other climbers in the area are to be commended for evacuating McLeod off the technical portion of the route without further incident or additional insult to McLeod's injuries. The "Code of the Mountains," where climbers on other teams drop what they are doing to assist an injured climber, is alive and well at Longs Peak! (Source: Jim Detterline, Mark Magnuson, Mark Ronca—Rangers, Rocky Mountain National Park)

FALLING ROCKS AND OBJECTS, INADEQUATE COMMUNICATION
Colorado, Eldorado Canyon, Bestowal Crack

I was on Werk Supp at the belay after the first pitch when a party on Bestowal Crack decided to set belay anchors in the Choss Gully (5.5-5.6 rated last pitch of Bestowal Crack). They managed to rain down a bucketful of pebbles and a brand new (with price tag and unslung!!!) Friend without calling, "Rock." Unable to contact the party in trouble and with no communication attempt being made by them, my partner and I decided to retreat from the climb by rappelling down to the top of "March of Dimes" pitch below us. We decided to do this because of the increasing amounts of debris striking us and bouncing on the rock around us. After my partner Vince (a very experienced climber from Switzerland) had made the rappel, I watched in horror as a 3'x4'x6' block slid down the gully (the second pitch of Werk Supp) and collected everything out of the gully—marked "slot" in Rossiter's "Rock Climbing Eldorado Canyon." At the end of the gully where the second pitch of Werk Supp starts, everything became airborne as it then fell to the roadway below, clearing my partner at the anchors below by a few feet. The main block broke in two pieces mostly going over the road with a piece striking (but not severely injuring) a father of a family of five walking along the road. Had a vehicle been on the roadway, it would have surely been destroyed.

The party causing the incident—a man and woman—then rappelled the entire route, throwing rope on two parties below as they descended without calling.

Analysis

The proximity of the roadway to the Bestowal provides ample opportunity for observers and waiting parties to be injured by falling gear and/or rock.

The party in distress failed to communicate their situation to any other party. Assistance could have been easily gained from my party or another party as there were over ten parties on the various routes of the Bestowal that day. Pride is probably at fault here with the gentleman failing to call for assistance in the presence of his female partner.

I hate speculation, but the best account I have from a local climbing shop (Neptune's in Boulder) faults several anchors all placed behind the large, already loose block. When the anchor(s) failed under weight of the man, he fell and was only arrested by the woman tackling him on the ramp between P3 and P4 with no anchors remaining on their rope. Still roped together, she would have saved both of their lives.

Unfamiliarity with the route and a lack of understanding of the forces generated outward by a loaded cam are probable the core issues. All were multiplied by the other issues previously mentioned.

I was wearing a helmet that day and always do now for my own safety and to make others around me feel comfortable wearing their helmets. I can only thank the Lord that we did not continue along the route, as we certainly would have been killed by the block that washed the gully. I no longer climb below or nearly below any other parties. (Source: Ray Bloch)

FATIGUE—FALL ON ICE, INEXPERIENCE
Colorado, Rocky Mountain National Park, Main Falls

On December 8 about 1000, Aaron Shupp (22) fell 20 to 30 feet while leading the Main Falls Route (I WI 4) at Hidden Falls. Shupp said that he was about 10 feet beyond his last ice screw when he began to "sketch out." He attempted to place protection but could not hang on. Shupp ran out of strength and purposely submitted to a leader fall, alerting his belayer that he was coming off. As he fell, Shupp left both hand tools and a glove dangling from his last position on the ice. Shupp caught a mushroom of ice with his right crampon and heard a loud "crack." He then impacted on the midway ledge of the water ice formation and was stopped by his previous ice screw. Shupp's belayer, Seth Ian Friedly (age unknown), lowered Shupp to the base of the climb, where they determined that Shupp was unable to walk.

Friedly left the scene to get his pick-up truck and drive it around the locked gate off-road and onto the closed road at the Deerhaven Trailhead. Friedly failed to notify authorities of the accident even though the Wild Basin Warming Hut at the summer trailhead was open and staffed. The three-person Scott Dimetrosky party stayed at the scene and waited for Friedly to return. Upon Friedly's return, they assisted Shupp down the talus slope to trail, where two other ice climbers took over in assisting Shupp and Friedly back to Friedly's vehicle. Shupp and Friedly were met at the vehicle by ranger Eric Gabriel. They refused medical treatment and transport. Friedly transported Shupp to Boulder Community Hospital in his personal vehicle.

Analysis

To lead an ice climb is a serious proposition. Modern hand tools, crampons, ropes, and ice protection have improved the safety aspects of the sport considerably, but these are no substitute for experience, good judgment, and proper physical conditioning. Because ice conditions on the same route change considerably from day to day (and even within the same day), may vary on the climb, and and are difficult to assess, it is recommended that beginning ice climbers receive professional instruction and afterwards apprentice themselves to an experienced ice climber before attempting to lead ice. In general, leading an ice climb is much more complicated by objective hazards than is leading a rock climb. Falling on ice should be avoided at all costs due to the inherent hazards of having all the sharp metal points around the leader moving at velocity, as Shupp discovered when his crampon caught on ice and injured his leg.

Shupp had minimal experience and lacked sufficient strength to safely lead Hidden Falls. Some "tricks" that experienced ice climbers have employed upon finding themselves in a similar situation have been 1) catch a loop of rope over top of a securely-planted ice ax as a temporary belay whereas the belayer could tighten up on the leader and allow for the placement of protection; 2) attach an ice tool to the harness of the leader with a fifi hook or carabiner to allow the leader to place protection; 3) place a temporary fast piece of protection such as a spectre sling to allow the placement of a better piece; or 4) down-climb to the last piece of protection to avoid a leader fall.

Due to the inherent hazards of our sport, climbers should consider first aid training and should also be aware of their limitations in effecting a rescue. When interviewed by a ranger/medic at the trailhead, Shupp and his party said they did not have any significant medical training, yet declined assessment and treatment. Given Shupp's fall, this decision could easily have exacerbated any injury and, potentially, had significant consequences for the patient. It is very possible, especially when dealing with the victim of a long fall, to further injure the patient with improper assessment and treatment. (Source: Jim Detterline, Mark Magnuson, and Eric Gabriel—Rangers in Rocky Mountain National Park)

FALL ON INDOOR CLIMBING WALL—NO PROTECTION
Minnesota, Duluth, Vertical Endeavors Climbing Gym

Tom Upham (27) was climbing the wall with friends about 9:00 p.m. when the accident occurred in the Bananaz Family Entertainment Complex.

Upham said, during a phone call from the hospital Friday afternoon, that he was more than 20 feet up the wall when he pushed off to come down. "There was no tension in the rope to bring me down," he said. He crashed to the floor. He said he landed on his left side and slammed his head on the floor. Upham said he sustained injuries to his head, neck and lower back and an abrasion to his right arm from the rope.

Michael Skoglund, manager of Vertical Endeavors in Duluth, referred questions regarding the incident to Steve Boynton, general counsel for the chain of climbing gyms, who said that an internal investigation is being conducted.

"We're looking into the causes," he said. "What we do know is that the climber was climbing a route that was closed and he shouldn't have been on that route."

Upham, a sales manager for a Duluth business, said "Nothing was fenced off" and he didn't see a sign. He said a "handwritten note wrapped around the rope" was pointed out to his fiancee after he fell. (Source: *Duluth News Tribune*, no date)

(Editor's Note: There have been very few reports of indoor—or outdoor—climbing wall incidents. This one poses the interesting problem as to how information is communicated to paying participants.)

FALL ON ICE—ICE BROKE OFF, MISJUDGED CONDITIONS
New Hampshire, Frankenstein Cliffs, Cave Route

I reached the top of the headwall on the Cave Route—approximately 50 feet high. The poor quality of the ice precluded me from placing more than one screw on the climb. At this point the belay anchor was approximately seven feet up on an angled slope. This slope was snow covered with no ice, moss, roots, or anything to be found that one could sink an ax into. The front points of my crampons were in the ice on the top section of the headwall. There was a loud crack and that section of ice broke and peeled away from the rock. I fell approximately 20 feet straight down and hit an ice bulge with my feet. My ice screw was positioned just above the bulge. From the impact on the bulge, I was thrown a bit to the right and further down approximately 20 feet (the point at which the screw held). This prevented a direct ground fall. From there, I skidded approximately ten feet to the base of the climb.

My climbing partner was quickly there, and within ten minutes I was assisted by approximately 15 other climbers. My fractured leg was stabilized; I was kept warm and was carried out on a liter by the other climbers. I suffered a fractured tibia and fibula and some bruised ribs. (Nine weeks later, I am recovering nicely.)

Analysis

[I should exercise] better judgment when examining the quality of the ice. (Source: Rick Gauthier)

FALL ON ICE, INADEQUATE PROTECTION, EXCEEDING ABILITIES
New Hampshire, Frankenstein Cliff, Standard Route Left

On February 17, the strongest leader, Tom, had apparently done the first (crux) pitch just fine. The second leader, Jim, fell while attempting the 20-foot bulge above. He decked on one of the ledges and broke his ankle. Jim immobilized the ankle with ice tools and webbing and lowered him as far as he could. Their ropes would not reach the ground from the belay. They did not know how to do a tandem rappel. Several other climbers nearby talked the second through the lowering process until they could get the second on their rope.

An experienced climber from the Adirondacks was helpful, as was another climber who is a physician's assistant. Two members of the Bartlett Fire Department came with a litter perched atop a fat dune buggy tire to take him out. This litter made the carry-out process much easier in a single track trail.

Analysis

Standard Route Left is a climb that looks easier than it is. Many intermediate leaders are lulled into a false sense of security because of the much easier main Standard Route to the right. The curtains on this route, while short, are quite vertical and can often be brittle. Even on easy ice bulges anything can happen. Place ice screws in places that will prevent ground fall, even if the climbing is easy. Several accidents have happened here in the past couple years. (Source: Al Hospers)

FALL ON ICE—MEDIOCRE ICE QUALITY, INADEQUATE PROTECTION
New Hampshire, Frankenstein Cliff, Pegasus

On March 14 the climber started up the lower right side of Pegasus. This was the most interesting side of the climb at this time and it had been done many times. The ice was chandeliered and somewhat "funky." He was approximately seven feet up, in the standard "monkey hang" position with picks of both ice axes buried. They both ripped from the ice simultaneously. The leader fell and hit his left crampon on a ledge and stopped short, right at the bottom. He was immediately aware there was a problem and advised his partner to pack up the gear. After taking a number of Ibuprophen, he self-evacuated by sliding down the hill to the railroad tracks and hopping back to his car. He drove himself to Memorial Hospital in North Conway where his injury was diagnosed as a fractured heel bone.

Analysis

The leader was not high enough where he would normally have placed protection. In fact, the accident occurred so low that protection would likely have been of no benefit, and a fall from this height would most often cause no problem. Catching the crampon was pure bad luck. Sometimes accidents just happen, even to experts. (Source: Al Hospers)

PROTECTION PULLED OUT—FALL ON ROCK, INADEQUATE BELAY—ROPE DIAMETER TOO SMALL
New Hampshire, Cathedral Ledge, Retaliation

The leader, Al (30s), was climbing and was below the crux at the niche. He had just placed a cam and was yanking on it to test the placement when it pulled out. He lost his balance and fell striking the wall. He and his partner Tammy did not fall to the ground but were hanging just above a belay ledge of a climb to the right called Youth Challenge. A nearby climber rappelled to him and gave assistance and comfort until MRS members arrived on the scene. Three local guides lowered the leader to the ledge and splinted his leg. They fixed ropes across the tree ledge running across the middle of the cliff, and he was littered out with the assistance of local fire department personnel.

Analysis

Retaliation is a climb that is deceivingly difficult. It is a right-leaning dihedral that is rated 5.9 but is really a climb for 5.10 leaders. One must be comfortable lay-backing the dihedral and placing your gear down by your knees where you can't see it well at all. The leader fell just below the crux and swung into the wall. The belayer's hands were burned, which may indicate that she was not keeping the belay properly. They were also using a lead rope that was less than 10 mm diameter. This size rope requires significantly more attention from the belayer as it can run much faster.

We have seen or heard of several accidents over the past year where the belayer let the leader fall further than desired because of the use of a "skinny" lead rope. If you are using a skinny rope the belayer should pay close attention and be prepared to arrest a fall quickly. (Source: Al Hospers)

FALL ON ROCK—FAILURE TO CLIP INTO QUICKDRAW, WEATHER, INADEQUATE EQUIPMENT—SHOES
New Hampshire, Rumney Crags

Mark (33) and I have been climbing together for a few years now. I recently took a lead climbing course and have already led a few climbs. Our new friend, Hande (21), was interested in climbing and today was going to be her introduction to the sport. We decided to climb at Rumney, in New Hampshire. I had recently climbed there and even led a few sport climbs. It would be perfect for Hande's first day of climbing.

The day was overcast, but we set out anyway, hoping that the tree cover would protect the cliffs. We got to Rumney at 0930 and hiked to a nice 5.7 sport climb that would be perfect. A group was already there, packing up. They stated that it was too wet to climb and they were heading out. We decided to climb it anyway, as it was more of a steep slab climb. Plus, I had already climbed it a few weeks before.

I started the climb by 1000 and was two bolts up in minutes. Then I fell. No problem, Mark did an excellent job catching me, and I was fine. Hande was a little nervous, but we explained that I would set up a top rope for her. I proceeded back up the cliff, which was easy climbing with a few 5.8 moves on sharp rock.

Once I was in reach of the third bolt, about 20 feet up, I clipped in my quickdraw. The lower carabiner was hanging just above my head. My feet were on a few little nubbins, which made me nervous. My Boreal Zephyrs were not as sticky as I had hoped, and I had been having trouble with them for weeks. I pulled up on the rope, yelled, "Slack," and Mark dished it out. My left hand was on a sharp finger hold and my right was trying to clip.

I don't know why I couldn't clip that 'biner. I had three or four tries and just could not clip it. The next thing I remember was leaving the cliff and yelling, "Falling!"

Due to the slack I had pulled up to clip with, and the fact that my last clip was about 8 feet below me, I fell about 20 feet to the deck. I hit, butt first, on a rock that was slanted towards the cliff. As I hit the rope went taut and pulled me towards the cliff. Mark had instantly locked me off when I fell, but all that slack allowed me to deck. I ended up leaning against the cliff trying to catch my breath, as the wind had been knocked out of me. Mark came to my side and asked, "What do you want me to do?"

I said, "Ambulance."

I have been an Emergency Medical Technician for three years, two with my Intermediate certification, so my mind was racing with the possible injuries I had just sustained. I knew my mechanism of injury was significant and I potentially had some very serious injuries. I was thinking compression fracture of my vertebrae and a pelvis fracture—both very painful and life threatening.

I instructed Mark to piggyback me to the ground. I then taught him how to do a full trauma assessment on me to see if I had broken anything. Luckily, everything seemed clear.

Mark got a cell phone and called the local ambulance squad, Plymouth Fire-Rescue. I talked with them on the phone to relay my status and what they would need to extract me from the climbing area. Within minutes they were there. I was back-boarded and taken to the ambulance. I was then transported to Speare Memorial Hospital. X-rays showed that nothing was broken and a CAT scan verified that no blood vessels were torn. However, I had lost two units of blood somewhere and the doctors could not determine where. So, I was admitted overnight to the CCU (Critical Care Unit) in case something that was overlooked would cause my condition to deteriorate rapidly.

Luckily, I was discharged the following morning with an "A-OK" from the surgeon. I was badly bruised and had a very uncomfortable half-hour ride home. When I looked in the mirror at my injuries, I realized I had lost all that blood to my butt, as one side was swollen larger than the other.

Analysis

What caused me to fall? Was it just the failure for me to clip? Was it just the wet conditions? Was it because of my non-sticky shoes? Or was it the fact that, during breakfast, we had a long discussion about the fact that none of us has decked on a fall? Since I do not really believe in voodoo magic, let's look at the others.

I think three things caused my 20-foot plummet. The direct one was not clipping. For a few nights after my accident I would close my eyes and see that carabiner moving away from me as I fell. I just could not get the rope clipped in. To prevent this, I have set up a quickdraw on my gym where I clip rope in 5 times per hand per side every night before I go to bed. Practice makes perfect.

Also, why was I reaching for the clip? I should have climbed higher so there would not have been so much slack. When I fell, the slack included the rope from me to where the 'biner was and then back down. I effectively doubled my slack when I reached high for the clip. It almost killed me.

The two indirect causes were the rain and my shoes, which just don't stick. I no longer climb in the rain, and I purchased new shoes made with the newest rubber. They stick much better than my previous shoes.

This accident demonstrated to me that it is just a few mistakes that lead to a big fall. Three things caused me to fall that day, and it has taken three weeks to recover—a horrible way to start my summer vacation. It has also shown me the value of a good belayer. Yes, Mark did not catch me, but that was because there was too much slack in the system for him to catch me. He did everything right. Plus, he has the extraordinary ability to remain calm in a crisis situation. After I fell and was leaning against the cliff, I overheard him telling Hande what we needed to do. He spoke in a very calm manner and was definitely in control. If he had panicked I would have had to call the ambulance myself. I feel very comfortable climbing with him now because I know that, if something happens, I can depend on him one hundred percent. Faith and trust in your belayer is one of the most important aspects of climbing. Even if all your equipment works, if your belayer doesn't work, you'll have to yell at them from the skies above.

Every climber should have some medical training. Not everyone needs to go out and get an EMT certificate, but some level of medical training should be taken, such as a first responder course or even a first aid course. You never know what is going to happen. It is imperative to be able to not only bandage minor wounds but also realize when the injuries are life threatening. (Source: John Kettinger—25)

FALL ON ROCK, PROTECTION PULLED OUT
New Hampshire, Cannon Cliffs, Vertigo

Daniel Chaffee (20) was climbing on Vertigo. He was on the second pitch when he fell 70 feet when his protection pulled out. Chaffee was caught by his partner Ryan McKeon. He came within 20 feet of hitting the ground.

Luckily there were plenty of climbers in the vicinity to get things started and help with the carry. The Stokes litter was passed all the way down the talus by a continuous chain of climbers, Fish & Game, and Local search & rescue people. It took 40 rescuers nearly four hours to bring Chaffee down from the mountain. The accident took place around 11:00 a.m., and he was in an ambulance by about 4:00 p.m.

Chaffee suffered serious injuries, including multiple fractures of the leg, a broken jaw, broken arm/wrist, and facial injuries. He was airlifted to Dartmouth Hitchcock Medical Center and is expected to recover fully.

STRANDED, INEXPERIENCE
New Hampshire, Cannon Cliff, Whitney Gilman

On October 12, New Hampshire Fish and Game received a report of two individuals with a stuck rope on the Whitney Gilman rock climb. Joe Lentini and another EMS guide took the tram to the top and walked across to the top of the climb with a 300 foot static line. It was snowing and slippery. The other guide rappelled down. The climbers had ascenders but didn't know how to use them, so they were hauled up. Apparently their rope got stuck and they called for help on a portable Motorola. They were carrying a large American flag! (Source: Al Hospers)

VARIOUS FALLS ON ROCK (22 LEADER FALLS)—MOSTLY INADEQUATE PROTECTION, OFF ROUTE (2), RAPPEL ERROR, INADEQUATE BELAY
New York, Mohonk Preserve, Shawangunks

There were 24 climbing related accidents reported from the Mohonk Preserve this year. The majority of the accidents that resulted in fairly serious injuries were caused by inadequate protection—resulting in long falls; having too much slack in the rope—resulting in falling all the way to the ground and/or a ledge; or just impacting the cliff-face. In two cases, the falls were the result of being off-route on a more difficult route than had been anticipated. The rappelling accident was the result of an inadequate braking system, so the rope ran too quickly through the rappeller's hands, causing rope-burn.

Only two vertical cliff rescues were required. In both cases, climbers were evacuated in a litter with full C-spine precautions. In most other cases, the climbers were encountered, treated, and evacuated from the base of the cliff.

As seems to be the case with the previous several years, the average age of the climbers was 39 and the average degree of difficulty of the climbs was moderate AT 5.8.

The incident reports are very brief in terms of narrative, and therefore, no specific narratives are included. From time to time, as in the case of last year, reports are sent forward by the persons involved. (Source: From the Annual Report submitted by the Mohonk Preserve and Jed Williamson)

FALL OR SLIP ON ROCK, BELAYER ERROR
North Carolina, Crowders Mountain State Park, Gumby's Roof

Ringo Willoughby (31) and a female friend were top-rope climbing in the Gumby's Roof area on Crowders Mountain during the afternoon of Saturday April 21. Ringo was approximately 20 to 25 feet on route when he fell. His belayer was unable to arrest his fall. He subsequently fell to the ground where he broke his right ankle. A backpack and some resistance from the belay device seems to have slowed his descent, thus reducing the potential for further injury. Further investigation revealed that Ringo's partner was an inexperienced belayer and was taught how to belay prior to the rock climb.

Crowders Mountain State Park personnel and Crowders Mountain Fire and Rescue completed the litter evacuation of Mr. Willoughby. (Source: Jane W. Conolly, Park Ranger II, Crowders Mountain State Park, and Aram Attarian)

Analysis

This incident speaks for itself. Belaying is a fundamental climbing skill that is learned and perfected over a period of time. It is not a skill that can be taught (or should be taught) in a few minutes prior to beginning a rock climb. In addition, Mr. Willoughby was not wearing a helmet. Given the dynamics of the fall and the condition of the site where Mr. Willoughby landed, he is lucky that he didn't suffer a head injury. (Source: Aram Attarian)

NUT OR CHOCK PULLED OUT, POOR POSITION
North Carolina, Moore's Wall, Sentinel Buttress, Zoo View

On September 2, Ron Lantham (37) and friends were climbing Zoo View, (5.8) a popular climb on Sentinel Buttress. After completing the first pitch, Lantham, the leader, constructed a belay anchor under a large roof. He placed the belay anchor low and redirected the rope through a single piece placed overhead. His second fell, causing the upper placement to take the force of the fall, causing it to pull out. The resulting shock-load caused the belayer to lose control of the belay and drop the second.

The victim remained dangling on the rope for several hours after falling approximately 50 feet. Stokes County Mountain Rescue lowered the climber to the base of the wall around 7:30 p.m. The climber was airlifted to Baptist Hospital in Winston-Salem. He had a fractured ankle and possible internal injuries.

Analysis

Three important factors should always be considered when setting up any belay: Anchor (SRENE: Strong, Redundant, Equalized, No Extension), friction (belay device), and position (climber in relationship to his/her anchor and direction of pull). In this case, the leader ignored his position in relation to the direction of pull and the dynamics of a potential fall. The climber should have positioned himself below the anchor rather than above it, in either a sitting or hanging belay with the belay device attached to the harness. Redirecting the rope in a hanging belay can be done more efficiently, especially if the belayer is facing the anchors. Or the leader may have had more control if the belay device was attached directly to the belay anchor via a Munter hitch, GriGri, or other device suitable for this purpose. This approach may have given the belayer more options, especially in executing a belay escape and assisting his partner, or the leader could have climbed through the overhang and set up his belay— the preferred set-up. (Source: Aram Attarian)

INADEQUATE WATER—DEHYDRATION, EXHAUSTION
North Carolina, Moore's Wall, Sentinel Buttress

At approximately 1800 on June 6, I received a radio communication from seasonal office assistant Ryan Moorefield. He had received a call from Stokes County Communications that a climber on Moore's Wall had phoned 911 by cell phone to advise of an unconscious climber. I arrived at the scene (the base of Sentinel Buttress) at 1820 and was advised by the individuals on the scene that a climber, Jason Blevins (19), had been approximately 50 feet from the top of the climb when he passed out from dehydration and exhaustion (all Blevins had to drink this day was a half can of soda). Two climbers, Zack Blevins and Jesse Kale (not part of the climbing party), helped lower Jason onto a large ledge approximately 100 feet from the base of the climb. At this time Blevins regained consciousness but was disoriented. When I arrived, I spoke with Kale, who stated that Jason was conscious and speaking with no obvious injuries but requested water. While awaiting the arrival of Stokes Mountain Rescue, water was passed up to them via rope. Mountain rescue arrived at approximately 1845 and was led to a point directly above the climbers by myself and Ranger Joe Deppe. Mountain Rescue members rappelled to the climbers and assisted them to the base of the climb. Blevins was carried out to an awaiting ambulance by Mountain Rescue and Fire department personnel via Stokes Basket. Blevins was examined by medical personnel and signed a refusal to receive further medical assistance form. (Source: Craig D. Standridge, Hanging Rock State Park)

Analysis

Staying hydrated is an important consideration when exercising in any environment. This is especially true when climbing in North Carolina (or other temperate environments) during the hot and humid summer months. It's not uncommon to lose one liter of sweat during one hour of exertion. This incident reminds climbers to make sure that they remain hydrated throughout the climbing experience. Climbers should establish a water-drinking regimen in order to maximize performance. It's recommended that water be ingested prior to exercise and repeated every 15 or 20 minutes. Drinking a half can of soda for an entire day of climbing is clearly inadequate.

This rescue effort required over 140 hours of volunteer labor (26 people x 5.5 hours)! This is why climbers should familiarize themselves with basic partner and self-rescue skills in order to facilitate their own rescue. (Source: Aram Attarian)

FALL ON ICE, INADEQUATE EQUIPMENT—DULL CRAMPONS
Oregon, Mount Hood, South Side

On March 23, two climbers (both 22) were descending the South Side standard route on Mount Hood. One of the climbers lost his footing at the "Pearly Gates" (roughly 11,000 feet) and took a tumbling fall down the Hogs Back, coming to rest near the Devils Kitchen (10,300 feet). Injuries included various abrasions and a severely sprained ankle. Both climbers appeared to be responsible individuals and were both certified Wilderness First Responders able to assess and treat the injuries at hand.

Given the icy conditions and rapidly decreasing visibility, a call was placed to Timberline Lodge ski patrol to inform them of the accident. Both climbers were fairly self sufficient and intended to attempt a self-improvised rescue. Coincidentally two members of Portland Mountain Rescue (PMR) were in the immediate area and were informed of the injured climber by another party on the mountain. Due to the steep icy conditions and limited visibility, the climbers requested assistance with the evacuation from the PMR members.

Starting at the Hogs Back, the patient was lowered several pitches to the 9400 foot level near Triangle Moraine. At this point the terrain angle eased off enough to allow the patient to hobble off the mountain using ski poles with self-arrest grips as an improvised crutch. Two rescuers followed the patient using short tag lines as a belay. Once arriving at the top of the Palmer lift (8500 feet), a snow cat was able to provide transportation back to Timberline Lodge.

Analysis

Upon arriving at Timberline Lodge, the patient's crampons were inspected. The crampons were rented from an outdoor store and the points were very dull. It is conceivable that the dull crampon points were not sharp enough to bite in to the ice encountered at the Pearly Gates—and possibly contributed to the uncontrolled fall. Whenever renting mountaineering equipment, it is a good idea to thoroughly inspect the equipment and verify that it is in adequate shape for the conditions you think you may encounter.

Depending on the comfort level of the climbers, the use of a running belay may have been warranted considering the icy conditions on the steep slope. The use of a running belay certainly could have minimized the extent of the fall.

There are two additional worthwhile comments. First, when considering a possible self-rescue, it is important to be certain you are familiar with the terrain and any possible difficulties the rescue effort might encounter. In this instance the climbers could have lowered the patient over a cliff on the wrong side of Crater Rock, or descended the wrong side of mountain due to whiteout conditions. Do not attempt a self-rescue if it may cause the victim's condition to deteriorate more (or cause greater harm) than a wait for outside assistance with greater resources.

Second, in Oregon, Search and Rescue is the responsibility of the County Sheriff. The Ski Patrol is responsible for assisting injured skiers within the ski boundary and is not prepared to assist injured climbers high on the mountain. If an accident occurs on Mt. Hood, it is important to call 911, which can route the call to the appropriate resources in an efficient manner. Calling the ski patrol or a ski resort instead of 911 can complicate and extend the time needed to assemble a rescue team. (Source: Steve Rollins, Portland Mountain Rescue)

FALL ON ROCK, PROTECTION PULLED OUT
Oregon, Smith Rock, Crack of Infinity

On June 3, Rod Lucas (45) was leading Crack of Infinity, a 5.10b trad route rated three stars, requiring gear to three inches, according to Alan Watts' *Climbers Guide to Smith Rock*. Rod released his hold on the overhanging crux just three feet above his last solid piece and to his surprise, blew a #3 and a #2 stopper from the rock, falling 25 feet to a ledge and then another 15 feet to the deck, landing on his back.

With a broken ankle and pelvis, Rod was placed on a stretcher and lowered to the path by Redmond Fire and Rescue and a host of helping hands from fellow climbers. He reached the hospital about four hours after the fall.

Analysis

Rod Lucas lived near Smith Rock and climbed regularly with the pioneers through the 1970's and 80's. He has climbed Crack of Infinity several times in the past. He knows that he was not off route on the adjoining Friday's Jinx (5.7 R), described by Alan Watts as follows: "This sinister route put a half a dozen people in the hospital during the 80's. Oddly, the rock is solid and the protection reasonable, but for unknown reasons gear-ripping falls are a common occurrence on the first pitch."

Later, his friend Chris, a climbing instructor, inspected the route on Crack of Infinity and reported a double fist sized hole where Rod's first solid piece blew out of the rock. His second piece was deeply scored.

This is Rod's first serious accident in nearly 30 years of climbing, including all of the major peaks in Washington and Oregon. However, "Climbing is a sport where you may be seriously injured or die," as stated in the "Climber's Guide." (Source: Robert Speik)

FALL ON ROCK—POOR POSITION, INADEQUATE PROTECTION
Oregon, Smith Rock, Zebra

On June 23 Grant Pease (38) was leading Zebra, a 5.10a trad route rated three stars and requiring gear to three inches, according to Alan Watts' *Climbers Guide to Smith Rock*. Grant was high on the wall on a near horizontal traverse of a thin crack leading to the Zion route finish. He found that he was not able to protect the crack with his gear. He was about 15 feet out when, uncomfortable, he started to make his way back toward his last secure protection. He slipped off the traverse and made a 23 foot pendulum fall into the rock dihedral with great force. With a serious compression fracture of his ankle, Grant was lowered by his partner to their third belay anchor and then self rappelled to the ground. He reached the hospital about three hours after the fall.

Analysis

Grant Pease has been gym climbing weekly and sport climbing on summer weekends once or twice a month with friends for about ten years, leading to 5.9 and 5.10. He considers his experience level to be Moderate.

Grant suggests that climbers need to be very aware of the dynamics of a possible fall. While he was not uncomfortable with a total 15 foot vertical fall from his good protection, he essentially decked at the end of his 23-foot pendulum into the rock dihedral. (Source: Robert Speik)

FALL ON ROCK, CLIMBING ALONE—SEPARATED FROM PARTY, FAILED TO FOLLOW ROUTE, NO HARD HAT
Oregon, Mount Jefferson, Whitewater Glacier

On June 24, while descending from camp after a weather-shortened climb, Robert Stockhouse (28) decided to descend via a non-standard route rather than remain with his companions who insisted on descending the route they had used to ascend from Jefferson Park to their campsite. His friends were in communication with Stock house via Family Radio Service radios. He reported to be clear of bad terrain and would meet them in the gully the two were descending. They never saw him in the gully, and when they arrived in Jefferson Park, they could not locate him. They assumed he had headed for the car. When he was not found at the car, both companions returned to Jefferson Park and were again unable to locate him. As the weather deteriorated toward nightfall, they returned to the car and drove to a telephone to report Robert Stockhouse missing. The following day, his body was found at the base of a 70–foot cliff band.

Analysis

While he was an experienced mountaineer, Mr. Stockhouse was not wearing a helmet while descending steep, wet rock in unfamiliar terrain. He had taken a rope from his pack to use while descending but was not wearing a harness, so it is not known for sure if he was attempting a body rappel or "fast roping." The rope was found some distance above the subject, so it appears he may have fallen before rigging the rope to himself or lost his grip on the rope, at which point he fell. Radio communication from him indicated he had successfully negotiated the worst of the terrain, but when his companions failed to meet him, further radio communication proved fruitless. When found later, his radio was turned off, leading to speculation by his companions that he may have become irritated. (Source: Bob Freund)

FALLING ROCK
Oregon, Mount Jefferson, Milk Creek Glacier

While crossing the north couloir of Milk Creek on July 1, two climbers (both 32) were ascending out of the bottom of the couloir on firm snow. One was crossing the bottom of the couloir when a rock struck him in the forehead.

The evening before the climb, while filtering water from Milk Creek, they did not hear any rockfall. They began their climb at 0230 to avoid rockfall and benefit from firm snow conditions. When they approached the couloir shortly before 0300, the snow was firm enough for them to use crampons. They stopped to put on crampons and to rope up. Still, no rockfall was heard. At 0310, a rock was heard rolling down the couloir. In the darkness, it was impossible to see the rock, but T.E. heard it strike P.D. and turned to see P.D.'s headlamp flying down the couloir.

A climbing group of ten came to the aid of these two and called for help. P.D. was evacuated by a National Guard helicopter about seven hours after the accident. He had suffered a concussion.

Analysis

This accident appears to be just bad luck. The climbers looked for but did not observe any rockfall earlier in the evening prior or during the climb until the one rock that caused the accident. The climbers started their climb in the early morning to lessen the rockfall danger. They stopped before reaching the couloir to rope up and put on crampons so they could move quickly through the couloir. It is not known what actions P.D. took immediately prior to the rock striking him, but he was wearing a helmet, which no doubt saved his life. (Source: Bob Freund)

FALL ON ROCK, INADEQUATE PROTECTION
Oregon, Smith Rock, Lyon's Chair

On July 7, Christopher Ekstrom (22) was leading the first pitch of Lyon's Chair in the Morning Glory Wall area of Smith Rock State Park. Lyon's Chair is a three star route rated 5.11a and requiring gear to 3.5 inches according to Alan Watts' *Climber's Guide to Smith Rocks*. "The start of the initial pitch makes a popular 5.10c stemming jaunt" according to Alan. Christopher was about eight inches from the first bolt anchors when he came off the rock, falling 15 to 20 feet and twisting his ankle.

His friends continued to climb for a while and then assisted him down the path toward their car, a half mile distant. They were met at the Crooked River bridge by a State Park Ranger who drove Chris up the steep hill to the parking area. X-rays taken the next day showed a broken tibia, requiring a cast for seven weeks. He made a full recovery.

Analysis

Christopher states he was seven to ten feet above his last piece of trad protection, and he reminds everyone to watch their run-outs. This is one of many accidents at Smith Rock that would not have been reported had not the Ranger observed the slow, painful progress of the group up the path. (Source: Robert Speik)

FALLING ROCK, PARTY SEPARATED—CLIMBING ALONE, EXCEEDING ABILITIES
Oregon, North Sister

On July 10, three people, including Matt Gorman, were climbing the North Sister. The terrain became more technical than Mr. Gorman's climbing companions were comfortable with, so they proceeded back down the route of ascent. Mr. Gorman elected to continue to the summit alone. While on the west face of the mountain in one of several large, exposed, and unstable gullies, a large (500-800 pound) boulder slid out from under him. He said he then "rode" the rock a short distance before he was ejected off it and went end over end several times. He came to rest in a gully several hundred feet below the summit. His two friends heard him yelling for help and called 911 via cell phone.

The response was from Lane County (Eugene Mountain Rescue), with an assist from Deschutes Co. SAR. Due to the fact that we did not know the extent of the subject's injuries and that he was seven to eight hours away from ground search personnel, we elected to send in a helicopter for extraction.

Matt Gorman was wearing a climbing helmet, and that may have saved his life. Injuries were a broken finger, strained knee with various bruises, and lacerations. He also lost his backpack during the accident. This left him with no survival gear if he had had to spend the night.

Analysis

A need to be aware of the loose volcanic rock of the Cascade Mountains and the consequences of climbing solo and within your abilities are only a couple of the lessons that can be learned from incident. (Source: John K. Miller, Search and Rescue Coordinator—Police Services Division, Lane County Sheriff's Office)

HIKER DISAPPEARED
Oregon, Broken Top

On August 10, Danny Curran (24) left his younger brother at their Green Lakes pack-in campsite late in the day, saying he was going to climb Broken Top, the snow capped mountain summit just one and a half miles due east. The elevation gain is 2,670 feet, over friable volcanic rock, snow, and ice.

Several climbers' trails lead to the prominent north west ridge, which in turn leads to a very exposed summit block with a 1,000-foot drop to the Crook Glacier. Permanent snow fields and the Bend Glacier buttress the north side of this summit ridge. At the end of the summer, the snow fields and glacier ice had pulled back from the rock of the knife edged ridge leaving crevasses and bergschrunds of great depth.

Search and Rescue teams and local climbers searched for Danny Curran until November 18, when the weather deteriorated and more snow began to fall.

Analysis

Danny Curran had little mountaineering experience. He was dressed in blue jeans, a black down jacket, hiking boots, a knit cap and gloves. He had no pack with back-up gear, even though he was climbing late in the afternoon in weather that dropped below freezing at night. The five-inch snow pack of the previous week had turned to two inches of hard snow, making footing treacherous.

The obvious recommendation is that it is best to climb with others. If people choose to go alone, they should learn to be prepared. "A lot of people hike alone," said SAR spokesman Chris Nolte. "We were up at the trail-head today, and it was raining, and we watched people heading up there solo or in pairs,

wearing fleece and blue jeans—not prepared. It just doesn't make sense to me."
(Source: Robert Speik and Jeff Scheetz)

(Editor's Note: On June 17, Corwin Osborne, an older and more experienced climber, also disappeared in the Three Sisters Wilderness, prompting a search that ultimately involved about 250 people, 28 agencies, and more than 6,000 hours. Corwin Osborne, a Washington resident, without ice ax or crampons, had planned to traverse the summits of South, Middle, and North Sister—an elevation gain of more than 10,000 feet, and hike almost 40 miles across country in one day.

Again, we present these cases of hikers who get into mountaineering situations in the hope that there will be some educational value.)

FALL ON FROZEN SCREE, FALL INTO CREVASSE, FAILURE TO FOLLOW ROUTE, CLIMBING ALONE, INADEQUATE CLOTHING AND EQUIPMENT, INEXPERIENCE
Oregon, Mount Hood, South Side and Cathedral Ridge

In late August, Bob Considine (38) was visiting Oregon from Missouri. He had a guidebook and intended to climb the "Sunshine" route on Mount Hood. He parked his truck at Cooper Spur Ski Area and hiked up to the stone hut above Cloud Cap, spending two nights there waiting for the weather to clear.

On Saturday morning he crossed the Elliot Glacier and headed up the Snow Dome until he got stuck in the crevasses below Anderson Rock. He then descended back to the top of Snow Dome and spent the night. On Sunday he traversed and ascended until he made Cathedral Ridge, using a "big Bowie knife" to cut steps in the ice, then followed the ridge to the summit where he set up camp.

On the summit he used his guidebook to discern a route down the Southside of the mountain. Unfortunately he picked the wrong gully for his descent, instead doing a variation of the Steel Cliff that comes out just above the Devils Kitchen. He stated he thought he had "messed up" when he saw the Devils Kitchen, but he did not want to ascend back to the summit, so he kept descending off of the snow and on to a scree slope where he fell, ending up in a small crevasse above the Devils Kitchen. He explained he was able to crawl out of the crevasse and from there it looked best to him if he descended the east side of the White River Glacier. He then hobbled and slid from about 10,200 feet down to 8,900 feet.

Upon hearing voices on the west rim of the glacier, he called up for help. A passing hiker/skier made the initial contact and then contacted a ski resort groomer who was able to get a call out for a mountain rescue.
Analysis

Mr. Considine had some experience climbing in the Rockies, but never on a glacier. He attempted the climb without the use of crampons, an ice ax, mountaineering boots, or a helmet. He was climbing on a glacier and steep ice without the proper tools or knowledge for a safe ascent.

Mount Hood is notorious for poor rock and is extremely prone to rock fall during the summer months. In fact, Mr. Considine stated that at one point during his ascent, a microwave-sized boulder went flying by. It is for this reason that climbing Mount Hood during the summer months or when the loose rock is not firmly frozen together is not recommended.

Mount Hood summit climbers are requested to complete a registration form and a Wilderness Permit located in the Climbers' Register in Timberline Lodge. The Climbers' registration form provides rescue crews with important information in the event that a rescue is needed. (Source: Robert Speik and *The Oregonian*, date unknown*)*

(Editor's Note: This is another example of a hiker trying to become a climber. He was lucky to have been rescued. As Sgt. Nick Watt said, "He's the kind of guy when he gets down and out of the hospital, he ought to play the lottery.")

FALL ON FROZEN SCREE, INADEQUATE EQUIPMENT AND CLOTHING, INEXPERIENCE
Oregon, Three Sisters Wilderness, Middle Sister

On September 29, Pete Acker (39) and Jeff Soulia (22) were descending a steep snow and scree slope north west off the 10,040 foot summit of Middle Sister when Pete lost his footing and slowly started to slide. He was unable to stop himself and rapidly picked up speed. Rocketing down the rough slope, he "hit a rock outcropping hard and began to tumble through the air," according to his companion. He came to a stop in talus, with a shattered wrist, four fractured ribs, and a fractured clavicle. Jeff carefully made his way down the 300 feet to his fallen companion who was unable to move.

They used the meager clothing they had to keep Pete warm, and Jeff left for their car and cell phone, four hours distant. After about an hours descent, Jeff was able to attract the attention of hikers and a skier who was able to descend quickly down the Collier Glacier. The skier in turn came upon a hiking group that had carried a cell phone. Hours later a SAR team of four was inserted by helicopter on the east side of the ridge on the Hayden Glacier, about two hours distant from Pete. He was stabilized and finally evacuated about 2:00 a.m. on Sunday after a painful and cold afternoon and night high on Middle Sister.

Analysis

It had snowed about two to three inches on the prior Tuesday. While the weather was nice enough to entice the climbers to wear shorts on a sunny Saturday, the high elevation and wind had iced the snow and scree and made a dangerous slide a possibility. An ice ax quickly used could have stopped the initial slide. Ultra-light ice axes are a good companion on high summer hikes and climbs.

Had the climbers carried available light-weight aluminum 12 point crampons, they could have descended more safely and easily on the hard remaining snow of the season.

Jeff Soulia asks that climbers be advised to carry enough extra clothing to wait in one place overnight. Luckily, Jeff was able to borrow the extra clothing they needed before he returned to his injured friend.

Pete Acker, who has returned to work after four months, notes that while the cell phone they had left at their car would not work in the low lying trailhead location, the cell phone carried by the others worked very well on the slopes of Middle Sister. (Source: Robert Speik)

PULLED ROCK OFF—FALL ON ROCK, FAILURE TO TEST HOLDS, EXCEEDING ABILITIES
Oregon, Smith Rock State Park, Misery Ridge Mesa

On October 17, Brent Bishop (19) and his friend Jason (19) were scrambling the fourth class route to the top of the Misery Ridge Mesa at Smith Rock State Park when Brent pulled loose a hand hold near the top of the climb. He fell about 40 feet, breaking his leg and cutting his scalp. 911 was quickly called. Redmond Fire and Rescue assisted by Deschutes County Search and Rescue approached from the Crooked River below the Gully and performed a high angle rope and stretcher rescue descent to a wheeled stretcher and a waiting ambulance.

Analysis

Brent, who has been bouldering for a while, says he wants to learn to climb with ropes. He says he has more respect for fourth class climbing following his accident.

This is one of several scrambling accidents at Smith Rock. The volcanic scree and friable rock in various locations in the State Park contribute to many calls for assistance from Park Rangers and Rescue units. (Source: Robert Speik)

FALLING ROCK
Utah, Arches National Park

On March 7, a large rockfall occurred during a technical rock rescue training session being conducted in the Park. Seventeen people were attending the training. The rock, estimated to be between 30 and 40 feet long and weighing over one ton, fell nearly 300 feet from the top of a sandstone cliff. It struck a small protrusion near the beginning of its fall, causing a loud noise, then broke up on its way down. The noise alerted six people who were directly below, sitting down to take a lunch break. They scattered just before the rock hit the ground a few yards behind the lunch location and exploded. Two park employees were injured. Andrew Fitzgerald was knocked to the ground by flying debris and suffered a head injury and multiple lacerations; Lee Kaiser, who was not among the six, injured his leg slightly while trying to get away from the flying rock. Fitzgerald was treated for his injuries, secured to a litter, lowered over the side of a 100-foot cliff to a second team, then transported a quarter-mile cross-country to a waiting ambulance. His injuries turned out to be relatively minor, and he was released from the hospital later that afternoon.

Analysis

Rain had fallen off and on for several days prior to the training session. Examination of the release site at the top of the cliff revealed that a large sandstone flake had simply let go of the surrounding rock. The rain-weakened condition of the sandstone, an existing crack in the rock, and freeze-thaw conditions typical of late winter in the area are thought to have been the primary reasons for the natural release. The high-angle rock rescue training is a joint NPS and Grand County SAR session conducted annually before the visitor season begins. Those who were directly below the falling rock with Fitzgerald, and therefore had a "near death experience," were Murray Shoemaker and Nathan Plants from Arches National Park, Dan Habig from Canyonlands National Park, and

Bego Gerhart and Frank Mendonca of Grand County SAR. (Source: Jim Webster, Ranger, Arches National Park)

(Editor's Note: Engaging in "area security" helps to determine conditions that may have changed for many venues. In climbing, routes may change as a result of freeze/thaw cycles—both for rock and ice. Knowing the history of the snow pack is critical for understanding potential avalanche conditions.)

FALL ON ROCK, INADEQUATE PROTECTION
Utah, Indian Creek

During the first week of April, Paul Sullivan, Ian Herring, Matt Pinkley, Bill Saul, and I (40) hit the ground running on our first day. Really, Matt and I had never been in an environment like "Wall Street" near Moab, Utah, and we hit the first crack we came to like kids in a candy shop. At Wall Street the cliff comes right down to the road so the approach is, basically, opening the car door. We all climbed until the light started to fail and camped at twilight.

Next day we ran down to Indian Creek and got on some classics including Super Crack and Generic Crack. The climbing was so good that we decided to stay where we were for another day. On the third day we got on a number of hard routes (thanks to Bill Saul) including The Incredible Hand Crack. Towards the end of the afternoon I loaned some of my bigger pieces to a team climbing Keyhole Flake so they could get safely by the three-inch crack at the mid-section of the climb. As soon as they were down, I got on the climb with Matt belaying. The first quarter is a flake, and from about 30 feet up it consists of two parallel splitter cracks. I had placed my third piece, climbed over it, and set two cams behind the flake above me. I pulled up slack to clip, and that is the last I remember of the climb.

No flaming, no, "Watch me!" I flat out peeled without a warning and with an armload of slack. When the weight ("m") of my body had accelerated ("a") through the slack and the distance, I was above my last piece, and the force ("F") was too much for the placements behind the flake and they popped. F=m x a! As far as I can figure, the top piece dragged out through the sandstone after giving Matt a good tug and the second blew out completely, as it was very small. I hit a ledge a couple of feet off of the ground, shattering my right fibula into a few pieces and breaking my ankle. I basically broke my foot off of the bottom of the tibia at the ankle. The last few feet of the fall was taken on my back and head. The impact of my head on the ground actually smashed in the back on my helmet and gave me a nasty cut as well as a concussion. (When I looked in the mirror later, I had a black and blue imprint of a #4 Camalot on my lower back.)

When I regained consciousness, my foot was pointing about 90 degrees from normal, someone was holding my bloody head, and the pain was excruciating. I really cannot describe how much it hurt. While my partners said I was unconscious for less than two minutes, I remember about an hour total of the first six or eight hours after the fall. Either the blow to the head or my body trying to deal with the pain shut my memory down. Two people headed off in opposite directions looking for cell phone coverage to call 911 while someone put a bandage to my head.

I remember the sheriff's deputy being on site followed by the EMT people and some of the procedures such as the neck collar, backboard, and inflatable cast. They took me to Monticello, where the doctors said, "Can't help you," and put me back in the ambulance for Cortez, Colorado, where there was an orthopedist who straightened my foot but did not do surgery on my leg.

The next day my dear friends took me all the way to Alpine, Utah, to bivy with some local friends until I could get a flight out. Two weeks later I had surgery and now I have a stainless steel plate and seven screws in my leg. The break in the leg and the associated hardware is not nearly as bad—read "painful"—as the broken ankle and associated ligament and tendon damage, which will require several months of therapy. I also have some nerve damage that causes non-stop, red-hot-poker type pain that will continue for a couple months. My head, elbow, and left hand still hurt. I'm on crutches for 12 weeks, but I plan to be climbing by October.

Analysis

I have made some observations along the course of this episode.

WEAR A HELMET ALL OF THE TIME. I would be DEAD right now if I had not been wearing a helmet. There was no loose rock or anyone above me when I was leading or any of the other "normal" reasons that cause us to decide to don a helmet, yet I owe my life to that piece of plastic.

Don't be afraid to "sew it up" in the desert. While all of the slack I had out and the fact that the flake was flexible may have done me in anyway, more gear is better.

I am impressed to emotion with the kind attention and care given to me by my climbing buddies. They helped me with the climbing and stuck with me like glue as I went from hospital to hospital and then to Alpine, giving up precious climbing hours. I feel guilty about keeping them off the rock and am very grateful for their support.

Buy good health insurance. The ambulance travel in Utah cost over $2,600 alone.

Lastly. If someone had come up to me, say, three or four years ago and said, "Over the next few years you can climb in great places such as the New River Gorge, Moore's Wall, Seneca Rocks, and Moab; you can meet some great people, stand on fabulous summits, and enjoy the heck out of your free time, but, along the way you are going to shatter your right leg in a painful fall," I would say in return, "Sign me up!"

I am planning to get back at it in September. Aconcagua in February, Moab in May. Nothing about this little injury has dampened my enthusiasm for the vertical world. Rock climbing is worth it. What can I say? I am an addict. (Source: Mark McConnel)

LIGHTNING—POOR POSITION
Utah, Canyonlands National Park, Lightning Bolt Cracks

The incident happened on Thursday, April 12 at about 12:15 p.m. Peter Carrick (Assistant Manager for Pacific Edge Climbing Gym) and I (Pat Kent) were on

Lightning Bolt Crack. There were six climbers in our group: five from Santa Cruz, the others being Eric Malone, Kelly Rich, and Joe, and one, Eric Husted, from Colorado. Kelly and Joe were at the base of the route; they had decided not to climb the route. Eric and Eric climbed the first pitch before descending. They pulled their rope right as the lightning hit the spire. Peter and I were also descending.

When the strike hit we were both anchored at the belay. Although Peter led the first pitch, and I led the second, we moved the belay down to the Liquid Sky fixed anchors (an old hex and a webbing now stuffed in the crack. So, when Peter came to me (at the end of the second pitch), I had him move down to those anchors, then belay me over. When I reached him, he clove-hitched me into the master point. Less than a minute later he was stuffing a back-up stopper into the anchor to beef up our rappel anchors. Right, and I mean RIGHT, as he did that, a loud crack of thunder hit and my whole body flooded with electrical current; my right arm felt like it was being burnt off, and my vision narrowed to tunnel vision.

The next split second I looked to my arm, lifted it to see if it was still there, then looked to Peter and saw him slumped back in his harness completely motionless. I freaked. The snow was still blowing from the tempest that had hit us, I was wondering about how to do CPR, what was up with my arm (it was temporarily paralyzed), and were our anchors damaged. I was not doing any of this calmly. I yelled down to the others that Peter was unconscious—he was out for about two minutes, then thank god, he came to, moaning, and I needed help. I had the rack, so I beefed up our anchors and I built a separate one, which I used to clip the trail-rope in to. I was able to tie a figure eight on a bight with the one hand and teeth; then I clipped the tail into our main anchors. The rope had already been touching the ground before the strike. I yelled, "Lines fixed," and Eric Husted began ascending with an improvised set-up (tiebloc and prusik). After Peter came to, it was obvious that he was thankfully breathing and his heart was still pumping. But he was very delusional, and had erratic, fitful body movements. Even in the ten minutes that it took Eric to jug up to us, Peter was gaining some control of his motor movement skills. I had to hold him, though, because he was thrashing around so much. For me, Eric coming up to help us was the defining moment of the rescue. At this point the four other climbers who had already climbed to the summit, returned to the base and started heading down the talus. They came back up to the base when they heard the yelling. So, there were eight guys at the base. Out of the eight, Eric jumped on the fixed rope while the other Eric (Malone) checked his improvised set-up and started organizing the others into a first responder team. Husted, who is a father of a six-year-old daughter, had only a second thought before he heroically launched into the still-storming and obviously hazardous spire. When Husted got up he quickly added a 'biner above the master point of the anchor, put Peter on belay, and lowered him to the ground. I was able to rappel with my left hand and a back-up fireman's belay from below.

Once Peter was on the ground, the eight guys began assessing his injuries, taking down notes, and putting together a plan. Two guys went out and notified the rangers, who in turn notified an ambulance from nearby Monticello. Two other guys went and reconned an appropriate route for Peter to walk (!) out on. They found a great way to the southwest of the spire. Everyone else helped Peter to walk. Within three hours of the incident, Peter was in an ambulance. An hour later he was in Monticello at the hospital/clinic. Two to three hours after that, he was on a plane to the burn center in Salt Lake City.

Analysis

About the exit wounds: Some of the doctors believe Peter was just "splashed" with electricity (I certainly was), and didn't actually have an entry and exit for the current. Peter's capiline top melted on his body, both his elbows were bloodied, the fabric ripped on his jacket and polypro, and his cheek was also bloodied. He had many other small "holes" in his jacket where electricity had escaped. I believe Peter was more than splashed. When he was holding the 'biner with the stopper on it, I think that was a conduit for the current. The reason his elbows and cheek are open wounds is because he was placing a stopper, and those parts of his body had contact with the rock. The big tip-off though, is the mark on the rock where his torso had been facing. The mark was circular, clear in the middle, and "charcoaly" on the outside. I believe this is where the current exited his body and passed to the rock.

We're both damn lucky, and I'm glad to be living and thankful my partner didn't perish right next to me while doing something we both love. (Source: Pat Kent)

AVALANCHE, POOR CONDITIONS, INEXPERIENCE
Utah, Big Cottonwood Canyon, Stairs Gulch

On April 28, Martin Gleich (38), a doctor from Salt Lake City and Scott Dull (39), also a doctor, from Eagle River, Alaska, were killed in Stairs Gulch, a tributary of Big Cottonwood Canyon. The pair left the trailhead about 3:30 to 4:00 a.m. to climb Stairs Gulch to Twin Peaks with ice axes and crampons, rope and snowshoes, but no beacons (they did not own beacons). They did not return by their 11:00 a.m. planned return time.

That evening, a Salt Lake County SAR team walked up both Stairs Gulch and nearby Broad's Fork looking for the missing climbers. They discovered fresh avalanche debris in Stairs Gulch and quickly found Martin Gleich's boot sticking out of the snow about 100 yards above the toe of the debris. His head was buried about four feet deep. Medical examiners later determined he died by asphyxia. After finding Gleich's body, Wasatch Backcountry Rescue, a volunteer group composed of avalanche professionals from northern Utah ski areas, was called. They responded with personnel from Snowbird and a rescue dog. The avalanche dog easily located Scott Dull, about a ten minute hike and 500 vertical feet above the first victim. Although he was buried eight to ten feet deep, part of his fleece shirt was torn to shreds and it stretched out about ten feet, with part of it on the surface. Scott Dull had multiple fractures, and the medical examiner reported that he was killed by trauma.

Analysis

The evidence indicates that the accident occurred early in the morning when the pair was on their way up.

Martin Gleich's sunglasses melted out of the debris nearly a month after the accident and they were still in their case, indicating that the accident occurred on the ascent while it was still too dark to wear sunglasses. Scott Dull's pack melted out a month after the accident, and it appeared to contain an uneaten lunch.

They did not use Martin's cell phone to call from the summit. Scott's widow indicated that he often would often call her on a cell phone when he got to the top of a ridge or mountain, and she thought it was unusual for them not to call.

They were wearing crampons at the time of the accident, and Martin had his ice ax strapped to his pack, indicating that they were not yet on steep terrain. They both were using their ski poles. When they ascended they were walking on old avalanche debris, which probably would have been hard enough to warrant wearing crampons.

Human factors: Scott and Martin were old friends. They had climbed several mountains together, including Mount Orizaba in Mexico (19,000 feet), Mount Rainier several times, and Mount Baker. They had taken a climbing school on Mount Baker as well as an avalanche course. The pair was on a constrained time schedule, as Scott and his wife flew into Salt Lake City just for the weekend. Scott and Martin had stayed up late catching up and had awakened at 3:00 a.m. for their climb.

Both were extremely intelligent people who were otherwise very attentive of their personal safety. Although they had taken an avalanche course, their friends reported that they were still relative novices. Also, although they both kept very fit and liked to hike in the mountains, they were still considered to be intermediate climbers.

Recent weather: The first half of April was very snowy. From the 3rd through the 23rd almost eight feet of snow fell in the Wasatch Range. During this cycle, one large dry avalanche released in Stairs Gulch on April 8 and descended 5,000 vertical feet, stopping only 400 feet short of the road. These storms ended on the 23rd, only five days before the accident. Then the weather warmed dramatically. The last overnight freeze of the snow surface occurred three days before the accident, but that freeze was quite thin and short-lived. For the next three days, daytime highs at the same elevation as the accident were in the 50's. The night of the accident, the minimum air temperature was 47 degrees F. This was the warmest overnight low since September.

Avalanche conditions: Stairs Gulch is the steepest and longest avalanche path in the Wasatch Range. The upper section is composed almost entirely of 45-55 degree rock slabs. Very few skiers or boarders ever enter Stairs Gulch in winter, but climbers sometimes practice their alpine skills there in spring after the snow stabilizes.

The accident was most likely caused by a glide avalanche about 700 feet wide with a fracture depth averaging about five feet. The crown was around

10,000 feet in elevation, and the avalanche descended 3,700 vertical feet, running about a mile in length.

Glide avalanches are relatively unusual for Utah, but they do occur regularly each spring on the steep rock slabs in Stairs Gulch and Broad's Fork, usually in a time window of about two weeks after the dry snow turns wet for the first time of the season. They occur when percolating water lubricates the interface between the snow and ground, causing the entire snowpack to slowly slide like a glacier on the underlying ground, often over the course of days, until it suddenly releases. One can recognize them by gaping crevasses on their upper boundaries and a rumpled-up look on their lower boundaries. Glide avalanches are very difficult to trigger—even with explosives—and they tend to release more or less randomly in time, like a calving iceberg or icefall. These are the first known fatalities from a glide avalanche in Utah and possibly the first in the U.S. (Source: Bruce Temper, Forest Service Utah Avalanche Center. The full text of the report is available at www.avalanche.org)

FALL ON ROCK, PROTECTION PULLED OUT, NO HARD HAT
Utah, Little Cottonwood Canyon, Pentapitch

On May 19, Michael Thurgood (24), Alex Santy (17), and BJ Huff (19), were climbing Pentapitch, a 5.8 route on the south side of Little Cottonwood Canyon. Michael led the second pitch, belayed by Alex. As he approached the end of the pitch, the rope drag became difficult and he decided to down-climb a few feet to his last piece, a cam, to add a runner. While down-climbing, his feet slipped and he fell, pulling the cam and a nut. He fell 35-40 feet, ending up three feet below his belayer when his fall was finally stopped by his next piece —a sling on a tree.

His partners hauled him up to the ledge, then lowered him to the ground with a GriGri. He was conscious and able to assist in the lowering, keeping his feet against the rock, although he remembers nothing from that time.

Search and Rescue members met the climbers descending from the base of the route. Michael was immobilized in a bean-bag vacuum splint, lowered several pitches down a scree field, and then carried to the trailhead. He was taken by ground ambulance to the hospital. He is now recovering well and has returned to lead Pentapitch again.

Analysis

Michael had been climbing for six or seven years but had only been leading trad routes for around a year. He feels that the rope drag probably caused the cam that pulled to "walk" to a position that was less secure. The best cam placements are in bottoming cracks that do not allow any motion. Long runners help both by eliminating bends in the rope, which add to rope-drag, and by preventing forces on the piece, which can cause it to walk.

All in all, the climbers did well to self-rescue to the bottom of the route, speeding up the rescue considerably. Michael was fortunate to suffer only minor injuries, but probably could have prevented a concussion if he had been wearing a helmet. (Source: Tom Moyer, Salt Lake County Sheriff's SAR)

KNOT CAME APART—FALL ON ROCK, INADEQUATE PROTECTION
Utah, Ferguson Canyon, Mission Impossible

On July 19, "Dan" (25), and "Jim" decided to beat the heat in the Salt Lake valley by climbing in cool, shady, Ferguson Canyon. Dan scrambled around to set up a top-rope on Mission Impossible, a 5.9 crack on the Cathedral. He clipped quickdraws to the two bolts at the top. Then, concerned about rope drag on the rock edge, he extended the anchor with a single piece of tied webbing. It was a long way from the bolts to the edge, and he had only one long sling, so he did not back up his anchor. He threaded a figure-eight device onto the ropes and started to rappel. Shortly after he backed over the edge, the knot in the webbing failed, and he fell 50 feet to the ground.

Dan was conscious and alert but suffering from two open lower leg fractures and a fractured wrist. He was immobilized in a bean-bag vacuum splint and carried out to the Ferguson Canyon trailhead, where he was loaded on a Lifeflight helicopter and flown to the hospital.

Analysis

The knot that parted was a water-knot, or overhand follow-through. The knotted sling that came undone had held body weight before. Dan guessed that he had ten days of climbing on it before the day of the accident. He did not check it carefully before his rappel.

Water knots can fail by gradually ratcheting under repeated body-weight loads. The tails get slightly shorter each time it is loaded. When the tails have ratcheted all the way into the knot, the knot comes undone. The accident could have been prevented if he had rigged a redundant anchor that was not dependent on a single piece of webbing. (Source: Tom Moyer, Salt Lake County Sheriff's SAR)

STRANDED, INADEQUATE BELAY
Utah, Big Cottonwood Canyon, Bumblebee Wall

On July 21, "Pat" (31), successfully led Perseverance Bulge, a two-pitch 5.9 route on Bumblebee Wall, near the Storm Mountain Picnic Area in Big Cottonwood Canyon. He sat on the ledge at the top of the second pitch and put "Betty" (22), on belay, but he did not set up an anchor or tie in. Betty began following the pitch but soon took a fall, which forced the rope into the crack and jammed it. The two climbers were unable to hear each other from their positions. The leader was unable to pull rope up and the follower was unwilling to climb up with slack in the rope, so she waited on a small ledge with her weight partly on the rope while he attempted to free the jam. After about 30 minutes, they yelled for assistance to people at the nearby picnic area.

SAR team members hiked around to the belay ledge at the top of the climb. The first step was to secure the unanchored belayer to a nearby tree. One rescuer was then lowered to Betty, did a pick-off, and lowered her 200 feet to the ground. With her weight off the rope, a second rescuer working at the location of the jam was able to pull the rope out of the crack.

Analysis

Pat's most serious mistake was trying to free the stuck rope while standing at the edge without being tied in. Had he succeeded, he would likely have been pulled off his stance. Even if his top piece had held, the 30-foot fall would almost certainly have caused him to let go of the rope, and both climbers would have fallen to the ground.

If Pat had set up an anchor at the top of the pitch, either climber could have attempted to solve the problem safely. The two climbers were about 100 feet apart and the jam was about 40 feet below the belayer. If the follower had been more experienced, she could have prusiked up the rope to the jam and attempted to pull the rope out of the crack. Or, since the jam was only 40 feet below the belay ledge, the belayer could have tied off the rope and rappelled down on the free end to work on it. Or, he could have prusiked down the taut side of the rope. Although neither climber was carrying prusiks or a cordalette, they were carrying slings, which could have been used to tie a Kleimheist hitch to ascend or descend a taut rope. All of these options, of course, assume that the leader can construct a solid anchor. Since he did not, yelling for help was probably their best option.

The leader described himself as a 5.12b climber with 15 years of experience. The follower described herself as a 5.8 climber on her first multi-pitch route. (Source: Tom Moyer, Salt Lake County Sheriff's SAR)

(Editor's Note: Similar to the above, on July 25, two climbers were top-roping a short climb just a few yards from the road in the Birches area of Big Cottonwood Canyon when their rope became stuck. One was left hanging in his harness about 20 feet from the ground. None of the climbers present knew how to assist him, so they flagged down a sheriff's deputy on the canyon road.

A pair of prusiks and the knowledge of how to use them would have allowed the climber to solve his own problem in minutes instead of needing to call for a rescue.)

RAPPEL ERROR, ROPE FAILED—INADEQUATE EQUIPMENT
Utah, Millcreek Canyon

On August 16, "Jim" (28) and "Kirk" (32) set up a sport-rappel at a small crag in Millcreek Canyon. They used an old cotton rope from Kirk's toolbox and tied off natural features at the top of the crag for an anchor. About halfway down, Jim bounced hard during his rappel and the rope broke. He fell about 20 feet, crashing through a small tree on the way and glancing off his partner at the base of the crag. Kirk was able to grab him at that point and stop him from tumbling further down the slope.

Jim was secured in a bean-bag vacuum splint and lowered two pitches down steep scree to the Millcreek road. He is lucky to have escaped with only a broken ankle, abrasions, and lacerations.

Analysis

Kirk was watching the rappel from the bottom when the rope broke. He was certain that it did not break at an edge. We later tested the tensile strength of the rope at Black Diamond Equipment. The rope was one-half-inch in diameter (13 mm) and in poor condition. Nine pull-tests were done unknotted—over three-inch drums. Failure loads ranged from 304 to 378 pounds, with an average break strength of 352 pounds.

A rappeller can easily generate rope tensions around double body-weight with only a moderate amount of bouncing. It is extremely fortunate that the failure did not happen earlier in the rappel. (Source: Tom Moyer, Salt Lake County Sheriff's SAR)

(Editor's Note: It's nice to know that "old cotton rope" can do even this well. Whether the two fellows had much climbing experience was not revealed. Let's hope they didn't.)

EARTHQUAKE
Washington, Mount Index

Chris Olson (28) was exactly where you don't want to be when a 6.8-magnitude earthquake hits: Standing on a 12-inch ledge 130 feet up a rock wall.

"I thought I was dead," he said. "It felt like the entire rock ledge I was on was going to peel right off the wall and take us with it."

An experienced climber, Olson was halfway up the wall standing on a ledge and helping his girlfriend's brother, Jim Shokes, who was about ten feet below him on a much narrower ledge. Olson was anchored to the top of the wall by a rope but was vulnerable to falling if the rock gave way.

"I was trying to belay him up to me when the shaking started," Olson said. "The granite wall was rockin' and a rollin'."

Olson said Shokes yelled at him that there must be a train coming. The tracks are right below the wall, which climbers often call "Godzilla."

"But I knew it was something more than a train," he said. "I thought it was probably a rock slide because I've seen and heard them before, and it felt like that. But I didn't hear anything.

"Then I thought Mount Rainier was erupting. I've worried about that because I've worked at Rainier the past couple of years. But I knew it wouldn't be shaking that hard all the way up there." That's when it hit him: Earthquake!

"All you could do was hang on," he said. "I could see the rock I was hanging on moving in and out. I thought it was over for me." About 50 feet to the right, he saw the entire area being peppered with rock. To the left, about 100 feet away, a huge boulder came down the side of the rock wall and hit the railroad tracks below. Then all Olson could see was dust clouds bellowing up from below.

"It felt like forever hanging on there," he said.

He turned to look behind him and saw an avalanche on Mount Index, where a deep slab of snow and ice slid down the mountain to Lake Serene.

"There were little dust clouds popping up all over in the woods from rock slides," he said. "It really looked like we were getting bombed." Once the shaking stopped, after about 20 to 35 seconds, Olson estimated, Shokes grabbed the ledge Olson was standing on.

"He pulled himself up, and we roped together and rappelled back down the wall," he said. "At the bottom, we threw our stuff in bags and left promptly."

When they got to the bottom of the wall, Olson's girlfriend, Mary Shokes, and his four-month-old daughter, Isabella, had just come from town to meet them. Mary had climbed the wall earlier and was walking back to town with the baby when the quake hit.

"She said she didn't feel it, but she saw the houses shaking, so she turned around and all she could see was a big cloud of dust," Olson said. "She didn't know what had happened to us."

As someone who has taught at the American Alpine Institute in Bellingham, is a climbing ranger at Mount Rainier, and who works as a Safety Manager at the Mount Baker ski area, Olson thinks of himself as knowledgeable and prepared for emergencies and danger in the wilderness. This, however, caught him off guard.

After the earthquake, they decided they'd head home to check on their place. They found it in shambles. It is just a few feet from where a landslide took out some homes. But it didn't take them long to put the experiences of the quake in perspective. They were back in Index on Monday with plans to climb the wall several more times this week.

"After all that, I feel really lucky," Olson said. "It was scary, but it won't keep me off the wall." (Source: Doug Sanders, Everett Mountain Rescue Unit Washington Region and *The Everett Herald*, from an article by Leslie Moriarty, March 7)

(Editor's Note: Active volcanoes, earthquakes, avalanches, and interesting weather always make the Pacific Northwest a challenging place to climb.)

CLIMBING ALONE AND UNROPED—FALL INTO CREVASSE, INADEQUATE CLOTHING AND EQUIPMENT
Washington, Glacier Peak, Sitkum Glacier

My climbing group, which included Jason Cass, Janie Cogen, Jon Hayes, and Yoav Bar-Ness, left camp in Boulder Basin about 4:00 a.m. on May 27 and roped up at the base of the Sitkum Glacier. We could see several other climbing parties starting up the route behind us.

A group of climbers with no rope or rescue gear passed us while my team was roping up. We soon caught up to them where they had stopped near a hole in the snow with an ice ax beside it. Looking down into the hole, the group had found a man about 20 feet deep in a crevasse, bundled up in a bivy bag. The crevasse victim, Kurk Balin (30s), had been descending Glacier Peak after summiting late the previous day. He was traveling alone on the Sitkum Glacier following footsteps made by climbers earlier that day and fell into a hidden chevron crevasse about 50 feet north of a small rock ridge at about 8,200 feet in elevation.

My roped team arrived next at the accident site, fully prepared with proper equipment for crevasse rescue. We decided to work with Marty Johnson, from the first climbing party at the site—and who was a member of Seattle Search and Rescue, to extract the victim from the crevasse. Marty set up snow anchors and a Z-pulley with rescue gear provided by my rope team. I used my harness prusik attached to an anchored rope as a self-belay to approach the crevasse lip to communicate with the victim, who was amazingly uninjured and in good condition after spending the entire night in the crevasse. The crevasse was extremely over-hung on all sides of the two by three foot opening. Looking into the hole, the crevasse appeared to trend northeast from rocks to the south toward the middle of the glacier. I used the victim's ice ax, which was still at the surface, to pad the crevasse lip, and anchored it with a second ax. We hauled Balin's pack out first, then I lowered a harness down to Kurk. However, the harness had become tangled during lowering over the crevasse lip. After I got the tangles out of the harness, it took awhile for Balin to get the harness on securely, as he had trouble figuring out how to put it on properly—and needed some instruction. The hauling team (some members of my party and a couple other climbers) raised the victim to the base of the crevasse lip, about two feet below the surface. I lowered a double-length runner, which the victim grabbed with both hands, then pulled him out to about chest-level. Balin was then able to push-up on the snow with one arm as I pulled on the runner, and he was freed from the crevasse.

We were surprised to find that the victim was wearing blue jeans, a cotton T-shirt and a Gore-tex jacket, and that he was not hypothermic. By this time several climbing parties had arrived at the site and watched the rescue from nearby rocks. Another team had heated some water for Kurk, and part of that group accompanied him back down the glacier.

Analysis

Kurk said he didn't know there were crevasses on the route. I reminded him that he was extremely lucky. If the weather had been severe that day and/or no climbing teams been on the route, he probably would not have been found alive. Additionally, if the victim had been injured, an evacuation would have been quite difficult due to the relative remoteness of Glacier Peak. (Source: Chris Cass)

FAILURE TO FOLLOW ROUTE—WEATHER, FAILURE TO TURN BACK, INADEQUATE CLOTHING AND EQUIPMENT, DEHYDRATION, HYPOTHERMIA, FROSTBITE
Washington, Mount Baker, North Ridge

James Genone (25) and I began the approach to the North Ridge of Mount Baker on June 7. We had checked the weather and [noted that] a storm was expected. The route was reported to require six to eight hours from a basecamp, so we thought we had an adequate window.

We stopped at the American Alpine Institute (AAI Guide Service) to check on conditions and were told that there was some fresh snow on the route and that it was a little slushy at lower altitude, but that overall, the route was in good shape. We inquired about the weather and were told that it was expected to be okay until the weekend. This corresponded to our own research.

At our bivy below Heliotrope Ridge, we were passed by an AAI expeditionary course. They had just completed an ascent of the North Ridge and confirmed the report that soft snow made for slow going low on the route.

We began climbing before sunrise the following morning. The weather was clearly unsettled, with lenticular clouds over the summit, apparently high winds higher on the mountain, and scattered and gradually building cumulus clouds. The lights of Bellingham were clear to the west, and we hoped conditions might improve. We made rapid progress, as the boot tracks from the AAI group allowed easy travel. The weather gradually deteriorated as winds and clouds increased. James suggested descending a couple of times, but I hoped that the weather might hold long enough for us to summit and descend, and if it didn't I thought we would be able to find our way down.

Around 10,000 feet, the angle steepened considerably. I climbed up a rope length, but the wind was rapidly increasing, snow was beginning to fall, and visibility was deteriorating. We were close to the summit, but finding our way across the vast summit of Mount Baker and back down the descent route in these conditions was unlikely, and we decided to descend. Visibility was approaching zero, and windblown snow was rapidly filling our boot tracks.

Shortly into the descent, I lost our track on an exposed, wind blasted portion of the ridge. I guessed, and guessed wrong, and soon we were wandering lost in the jumbled chaos of the Roosevelt Glacier, to the east of the North Ridge. At one point while descending a 40 degree slope, my legs punched through into a crevasse. I was swimming up to my armpits in unconsolidated snow, unable to arrest myself, or make progress up from the lip of the crevasse. James anchored himself, and with tension I was able to extricate myself and climb back up.

I was convinced from my observation of the Coleman and Roosevelt Glaciers the previous day that any attempt to continue to descend would result in reaching a dead end, and that the only solution was to climb back up and traverse west until we hit the North Ridge. When we reached an area which I believed was close to where I lost the track, we took shelter by a rock wall. I noticed a moat filled with unconsolidated snow at the base of the wall, and quickly stamped out a trench for shelter. The wind was strong, so the trench was poor shelter. I was getting extremely cold. I began excavating a cave for better shelter. I was able to dig out a fairly comfortable cave and began to believe that our chances of survival were better sheltered in the cave than in wandering blind in the heavily crevassed icefalls of the Coleman and Roosevelt glaciers. This was probably a mistake. We most likely should have attempted to traverse west and find our line of ascent. We had no bivy gear, and our remaining food consisted of one Clif Bar. James disagreed and wanted to continue descending, but I felt that wandering around lost in the storm would be suicidal.

We made one attempt to break out during the storm, but high winds, cold, avalanche hazard, and no visibility convinced me that the attempt was futile and that we were better off in our cave.

On Sunday, June 10, the winds and snow decreased, visibility improved, and we decided to attempt to descend. Two to three feet of fresh snow had fallen. In order to avoid avalanche hazard, James wanted to descend the Roosevelt Glacier, hugging the rock ridge on its Eastern border. I wanted to traverse west to the North Ridge and descend the ridge. We decided to descend the Roosevelt but were unable to find a way through the icefall, so we bivvied that night in a crevasse.

The following day I was extremely weak. James had been eating snow and seemed in much better shape. I had always heard that eating snow was a bad idea, but I began to eat snow and soon felt much stronger. We climbed back up the Roosevelt Glacier and again bivvied in a crevasse. The weather had deteriorated again, and our spirits were low.

After a bad night, the day dawned with more snow and poor visibility. Then, midmorning, the sky began to clear. We immediately decided to begin traversing west until we hit the North Ridge. We ate the last of our Clif Bar, suited up, and started out. James had broken trail the previous day and was tired, so today was my turn. The snow was hip-deep. That is, I stopped sinking in when it reached my crotch, but it was certainly deeper. Probing with a full length ski pole yielded four feet of unvarying unconsolidated snow, and every step took a force of will.

In our dazed, sleep deprived, and dehydrated state we over-shot the North Ridge and traversed around to the south side of the mountain, descending gradually. Near the tree line we thought we heard voices. Soon I spotted Railroad Grade, which I recognized from an ascent of the Eaton Glacier as part of an AAI class almost ten years earlier. I hoped that there might be a class camped there now, and that was in fact the case. The two guides had first aid training and two surgeons were members of the class, so we were in good hands. They warmed and rehydrated us and arranged for our evacuation. The following day we were dragged down in litters until the weather cleared to allow us to be picked up by helicopter.

We suffered frostbite on our toes and hypothermia. James eventually lost half the length of nine toes, and all of one toe. I recovered completely.

Analysis

Climbing into deteriorating weather was the proximate cause of the accident. Using the map and compass we brought, along with an altimeter (which we did not bring), could have allowed us to plot a course up the ridge which we could have followed back down blind. Adequate clothing and bivy gear could have reduced the consequences. We should have attempted to relocate our ascent route as soon as we realized we were lost.

But ultimately, it was my reluctance to "bail" that led to the accident. Our lack of experience with the severity of Cascade weather was a contributing cause. I have climbed through storms without consequence in the Sierra and on Mount Shasta. I had summited Mount Baker in a whiteout uneventfully ten years previously. This gave me false confidence. We were on vacation with limited climbing days. This contributed to my desire to keep going. But I believe it was Don Whillans who said, "The mountain will always be there; the trick is to make sure you're still there too." (Source: William Folk—39)

(Editor's Note: Honest self-reports like this one are the most helpful for this journal. It should be noted that Folk's partner also sent in a report with basically the same description and conclusion.)

HANDHOLD CAME OFF—FALL ON ROCK, INADEQUATE BELAY, INEXPERIENCE, FAULTY INSTRUCTION
Washington, Wilkeson

On July 7, I (25) took S.P. (22), my girlfriend of a year, for a day of instructional rock climbing and rappelling. I have been rock climbing for four years and mountaineering on a half-dozen Cascade volcanoes. She had no experience doing either. S.P. is about 25 pounds lighter than I am.

After getting into harnesses, establishing an anchor, and setting a top rope, I began instruction on rappelling. Fifteen minutes later we successfully rappelled the 30 feet, and spirits were high. I was to climb first, and she was going to watch and belay me. As she was lighter, I tied her into a large, solid, dead log at the base of the climb, with webbing that ran four feet or so to her. She was using a figure-8 as a base-plate to belay from her harness. We established signals, and I began to climb.

About 20 feet up, while talking to her, I lost my handhold and began to fall. S.P. was at this point only two or three feet from the log, and the weight of my fall pulled the rest of the slack between her and the log tight, yanking her towards the wall. She instinctively put her hand up in front of her to protect herself from the wall before the webbing halted her. I felt myself begin to go from a slowing motion to picking up more speed. S.P. quickly recovered and grabbed the rope, squeezing it tight before remembering to lock it down. By the time I had reached the ground, she had received second degree burns to her hands, and they had begun to contract.

Analysis

I had taught several people to climb and rappel, but this was slightly different, as this was someone I had an emotional attachment to. Whether this affected my decision making abilities I do not know, but it is a possibility. There is little substitute for proper instruction from an unattached person. I had anchored her to the log, but I had failed to mention to her to keep the anchor line to her harness taut. A better possibility may have been to establish the anchor and belay from the log. As she was new to the sport, she was not prepared for the jerk when I began to fall. After losing control of the rope, she did her best to regain a handhold, unfortunately gripping it above the belay device. I am happy to say since then S.P. and I have climbed in several other areas, to include the Gunks, without incident, and she and I have grown to enjoy the sport together. (Source: 1LT Michael Wissemann, 86th Combat Support Hospital)

FALLING SNOW BLOCK
Washington, North Cascades

On July 24 at 2:00 p.m., National Outdoor Leadership School Instructor Jon Stamp and five students left their camp on the saddle between Dome and Dana Glaciers. They were traveling in two rope teams of three, wearing helmets and carrying light day packs. They were headed west to scout a route for the next day's travel beyond Spire Creek. The group, led by Gabe (who was to be "leader of the day" on July 25), traversed the slope from camp and then descended on moderate to steep snowfields, ranging from 28-35 degrees at the steepest parts. The slope was interspersed with boulders and small rock bands. Snow conditions were good for this descent, with easy plunge-stepping and three to four inch boot penetration. This was Gabe's third time route-finding in similar terrain on this course. A running belay was not deemed necessary, as the slope angle, snow conditions, and students' experience on similar slopes made the probability of a "fall" low. The ability of each of the students to self-arrest would be sufficient to hold a "fall" if one should occur. The group did decide that running protection (anchors) would be necessary the next day when they traveled this route with full backpacks and firmer snow conditions of the early morning.

At 3:30 p.m., the roped teams "parallel parked" next to each other to discuss and locate their travel route for the following day. After making a plan, they decided to head back to camp, with the team of Bob, John S. and AJ leading, followed by Dan, Josh and Gabe (at the end). The first roped team had begun moving back up the slope towards camp and the second roped team had just spread the rope out between them and were preparing to move up when they heard a loud sound like rock falling. After John S. yelled "ROCK!" the students on the second roped team looked up to see a block of snow "the size of a refrigerator" heading towards them over a rise and out of the clouds from above.

The block's trajectory appeared to be at an angle to the fall line, coming from climber's left across the slope toward the right. The front rope team was out of the path by 35 yards to the right of the block. Dan saw that the block would go to his left and that he was out of its direct path. He then went into self-arrest. Josh saw the block. It appeared to be coming directly at him. He jumped to his right (facing the slope) and attempted to get into self-arrest position. Gabe saw the block and thought it would pass right between him and Josh. He jumped four steps to his left and was in self-arrest when the block hit the rope between him and Josh. Gabe thinks it was possible the rope was taut between them.

All three students felt an enormous tug and were yanked out of their respective positions, into the air, and then onto their backs, sliding and being pulled downhill. They were dragged down-slope approximately 200 yards, through an area where rocks were protruding through the snow. The rope team stopped sliding/tumbling after the snow chunk dislodged from the rope and continued downhill.

Dan was up on his feet almost immediately and was fine, except for a minor injury to his left elbow. Josh (a paramedic for six years) disentangled himself from the rope and made a scan of himself. He felt bruised and had pain in his left foot. He left his boot on, then looked over to Gabe.

Josh saw that Gabe was conscious and lying on his back on the snow, looking up and moaning and groaning. One boot was missing, his pack was off, and he had blood on his face and on the snow around him. Josh crawled over to Gabe and initiated a primary survey, which revealed that, "Gabe was alert and oriented, looked 'shocky' and was yelling and crying out in pain." A thorough secondary assessment from Josh revealed that Gabe's chief complaint was pain in his lower back and right chest wall. Gabe was lucid though more animated than usual, and Josh did not think he had lost consciousness.

At this point, John S. unclipped from his rope team to assist in the rescue and sent students Bob and AJ to notify the rest of the course. He told them to get Andy (the Course Leader), the drug kit, the radio, and to keep themselves safe while doing it.

Meanwhile, the primary rescuers dug a more secure and protected platform, and then John and Dan (and later Josh) dragged Gabe across the snow approximately 30 yards to the new location. Josh and John worked together to provide medical care for Gabe. They kept him immobilized for potential spinal injury, monitored his vital signs, and kept him comfortable until more help was available.

At 4:30 p.m., the entire group convened at the incident site and set up a station ten yards further right on the slope to provide additional support. At 5:15 p.m., Andy contacted a private pilot, Gary Larson, with a radio message stating "medical emergency requiring helicopter evacuation…. Alpha with a back injury." (Alpha = Critical, single life-threatening injury or illness, urgent response required.) By 6:00 p.m., the group received notice via radio that a helicopter would arrive in two hours. A team of Andy, John S., Gabe, Josh, and Lisa stayed at the incident site while the rest of the group was sent back to camp.

At 8:00 p.m. a helicopter from Whidbey Island U.S. Naval Air Station arrived and hovered overhead. A medic, rescue swimmer, and litter were lowered to assist in the rescue. They hoisted Josh via seat and chest harness, then packaged Gabe onto the litter and hoisted him into the helicopter. At 9:00 p.m. the helicopter departed the scene and arrived at Skagit Valley Medical Center in Mount Vernon, WA, at 9:30 p.m. Gabe's injuries included a fractured pelvis, three fractured lumbar vertebrae, and a pneumothorax.

Analysis

Weather and Environmental Conditions: It had rained in the morning, followed by mist, and the weather was slowly improving throughout the day. The group left camp in low visibility conditions. As they descended the slope they came out of the clouds. Visibility gradually improved during the afternoon with patches of sun showing through. Instructors estimated the air temperature to be about 45 degrees, and when the sun periodically came out it would become warmer. The slope aspect is southwest. There were no cornices on the ridge top or other indications of instability in this particular section of the slope.

Appropriateness of this terrain for these students: Josh, AJ, Bob, and Dan stated that they were comfortable on the slope and had traveled on steeper slopes with heavier packs earlier in the course. Gabe had led roped teams on similar terrain earlier in the course. John and Andy were confident in Gabe's route-finding ability and felt he made good decisions on that day. He chose the most obvious and least steep route of the options available. The instructors say they would have taken the same or similar line.

Appropriateness of the practices and procedures used while negotiating this terrain: Was the lack of running protection a factor? The lack of running protection (anchors) is appropriate in this case. Factors supporting this decision include the student's experience on this type of terrain, the slope angle (moderate to steep), the relative softness of the snow (good footing), the level of supervision provided by John, and the probability of one of the group members falling being low. Most likely if an anchor were in place to arrest a fallen climber, it would not have held the force from the sliding snow block.

Was being roped up a factor? The group was using standard mountaineering practices for travel in this type of terrain. Many of the same practices for placing running protection are considered for whether or not to rope up. Because of the dynamic nature of travel in the Cascades, groups continuously move over varying terrain. Any one travel day may call for situations that demand the use of running protection, fixed lines, fifth-class belay, or none of these. It is common for groups to move between technical sections while remaining roped up. Factors to consider include the consequences and likelihood of a fall, including: the run out, slope angle, consistency of the snow, levels of experience. If the slope is considered "mellow" enough (low angle) to have a low probability of a fall, groups will often travel through the terrain remaining roped up, because to unrope for all of these situations throughout the day would be impractical. This would take a tremendous amount of time and the groups would not get very far and possibly expose them to other hazards.

Another factor is the reliability of students being able to self-arrest on their own. Instructors will often place themselves on a rope team with less strong members in order to provide a backup to the students' self-arrest capabilities.

Nonetheless, if the group had not been roped up, the outcome would likely have been a "near miss" and not an incident. However, the practice this group was using was acceptable in this case. They were prepared to place protection at any moment, and were constantly analyzing the terrain around them to see if it was needed.

Hazard assessment: Was the limited visibility a factor? The conditions of limited visibility are common this time of year in the Cascades, and it was appropriate for them to be traveling under these circumstances.

As the rope teams were traveling through this terrain just before the incident, they had enough visibility to see that there was no potential rock, ice, and snow fall zones on the slopes immediately around them. The previous day in clear weather they were able to view the route from Dome Peak and identified potential rock/snow fall areas on slopes about a half-mile further west of the incident site. These particular slopes had no bearing on the incident. Gabe carefully selected the route with supervision from John. Gabe chose an appropriate route.

The day after the incident, the rest of the group passed through in clear conditions. Andy confirmed that the snow block was not obvious and would not have been identified as a hazard, had the group been able to see above them the day before. This chunk of snow broke loose from a snow slope that met with a rock wall, and showed no indication that it was separate and had the potential to come down the slope.

Had the rope teams been able to see the snow chunk when it first dislodged, they feel they would have reacted differently to it. It is difficult to speculate on all the "what ifs." The snow chunk was unpredictable in that it was moving very quickly, it was not following the "fall line," and there were terrain features (i.e. changes in slope angle and direction) that obscured the block for part of its path from the rope team below.

Gabe, Josh, and Dan all saw the block coming down after it had passed over a rise, before it hit their rope. They all reacted to it by moving (a few steps in each case) and going into self-arrest position.

This was clearly an accident caused by an act of nature. This group happened to be in the path of the sliding snow block. This was a random and unforeseen event, though one that should not be completely unexpected while traveling in steep, snow-covered terrain.

There were no contributing factors, other than being in the path of a falling object, that can be deemed as the cause of this accident. The course was traveling in reasonable terrain and conditions. They were keeping in line with NOLS Accepted Field Practices and general mountaineering practices. The response to the incident was handled well.

We will use this incident as a case study for mountaineering staff. (Source: Drew Leemon—NOLS Risk Management Director and Rachel Knapp—NOLS PNW Mountaineering Program Supervisor)

HEART ATTACK
Washington, Mount Rainier

In early August, Lawrence "Laury" Minard (51), a Seattle native who had moved to London to edit and write for *Forbes Global Magazine*, collapsed and died around 12,000 feet up Mount Rainier during a guided climb.

The Pierce County Medical Examiner's Office on Friday reported Minard died of arteriosclerotic cardiovascular disease, or ASCVD. The condition occurs as fatty plaques build up on artery walls, limiting blood circulation and placing too much strain on the heart. Mountain guides who fought for 45 minutes to revive Minard said he stopped breathing soon after his collapse and never regained consciousness.

Minard's collapse occurred while he was climbing with a guided party up Disappointment Cleaver, an outcrop of 45-degree rock bordering Rainier's Emmons Glacier.

Guides with Rainier Mountaineering Inc. say Minard complained he was having difficulty catching his breath and needed to rest. He unclipped from the climbing rope and sat down, but he collapsed and stopped breathing minutes later.

RMI guides halted the climb and performed CPR and other emergency measures, said Peter Whittaker, Operations Manager for RMI. The efforts were witnessed by the other RMI clients, including Minard's 16-year-old daughter, Julia. Minard's body was later flown off the mountain.

Park rangers say the zig-zagging route up the Cleaver is usually the steepest and most exhausting portion of the most popular route up 14,410-foot Mount Rainier.

"It's generally a spot where climbers recognize whether they're going to make it or not. The top of the cleaver is a common spot for people to turn around and head down," said Mike Gauthier, lead climbing ranger at Mount Rainier National Park. Climbing the mountain "is still really an almost extraordinary effort for people who are at a reasonable fitness level," Gauthier said. "At the top, they're wasted, they're tired—particularly when they're making a two-day ascent."

Deaths involving heart attacks are virtually unheard of among the nearly 100 people who have died climbing Mount Rainier, its satellite Little Tahoma, or the park's lower peaks. This appears to be the first known case of a climber dying from a heart ailment high on the peak, according to park records. The only death high on the peak thought to have been caused by a heart attack or stroke occurred March 19, 1989, when 54-year-old Wenatchee pilot William E. Saul flew directly into Rainier's sheer Willis Wall. Saul's body was never recovered. (Source: *Bergschlawiner,* August 4)

FALL INTO CREVASSE, WEATHER
Washington, Mount Baker, Coleman Glacier
Rescuers reached two seriously injured climbers on Mount Baker and were bringing them down the mountain in difficult weather conditions Monday morning.

The drama began on Sunday, September 2, about 11:30 a.m. when one climber was killed and three others were injured after falling into a crevasse. The fall happened at the 8,600-foot-level of Coleman Glacier on the western flank of the 10,775-foot peak.

Whatcom County Search and Rescue crews and personnel aboard a helicopter from the Whidbey Island Naval Air Station located the group Sunday, but the chopper was unable to land because of the high altitude. A 42-year-old man with minor injuries was able to get off the mountain, and ground crews reached the two more seriously injured people on Monday, sheriff's deputies said. Foggy weather made another helicopter attempt impossible.

Identities and hometowns of the injured and dead were being withheld. The two injured climbers are a man with back and leg injuries who was camped out at the base of the glacier at the 6,500-foot level and a woman with back and neck injuries who was at the 7,000-foot level. (Source: Dispatch from KOMO-TV, on September 3rd from Seattle)

(Editor's Note: No other details were forthcoming on this accident. The report is included because of the fatality.)

FALL ON ROCK
Washington, Snowqualmie Pass, Chair Peak
On September 8, Chad Engstrom (23) tumbled about 600 feet down a 45-degree rock slope while climbing with his uncle, who saw the accident. Rescuers ran out of daylight and planned to return to the site today to recover the young man's body.

The pair were about two-thirds of the way up the east face of 6,238-foot Chair Peak, about two miles north of Interstate 90. After the two had reached an overhanging horizontal band of granite about 150 feet from the summit, they unroped and started scrambling up the loose rock, said King County deputy Randy Potter. The uncle, a less-experienced climber from Sammamish, grew uncomfortable and stayed behind. Shortly afterward, he heard rock fall, then saw his nephew fall, Potter said.

Mountain rescuers said the accident occurred right next to a much easier route the Seattle-based Mountaineers frequently use for training. The route the two were on was moderate in technical difficulty—5.5, but other experienced climbers said it's a tricky one to safely navigate.

Another party of climbers, Webster, Peter and Scott Bergford, all of Olympia, called 911 on a cell phone about 1:00 p.m. when they came across the climber's shredded pack, its gear strewn about the loose scree basin below the peak. A few yards away, they saw the body.

The uncle rappelled down from his perch but left his rope hanging from the anchors. The Bergfords freed the rope, gathered the dead climber's gear, and built a memorial cairn to help rescuers locate the body.

They waited until early evening for searchers to arrive, then headed down the trail at dusk when no one came. Rescuers had been forced to abandon their efforts throughout the afternoon while they responded to two other accidents. (Source: Craig Welch, *Seattle Times* staff reporter, September 9)

LOST CLIMBERS—WEATHER, OFF ROUTE, INADEQUATE EQUIPMENT
Washington, Silver Peak

On September 25, a party of two males attempted to climb Silver Peak on a very wet, foggy day. Part way up the ridge from Lake Annette, they started to get into the open rock scree, decided that conditions were too bad, and turned around. As they started back down, they got off route and ended up cliffed-out. They pulled out their trusty cell phone and called 911. Officer Sheridan called Seattle Mountain Rescue member Doug Caley at his office to see if he could talk the two climbers down.

At 1715, Caley called them and talked to them on their cell phone. They had a GPS unit and gave their coordinates. Caley plotted the coordinates and saw that they were basically on the route. From their description of their location and their plot, Caley was able to advise them to move right to regain the route. They checked back in 15 minutes, and their new coordinates showed that they had moved half the distance to Lake Annette. At 1750 they called and reported they were at Lake Annette on the trail. Since they did not have lights and there was just a little over an hour of daylight to travel the 4.5 miles to the trailhead, it was suggested that they get off the phone and start moving quickly down the trail. At 1910 they called and reported that they had made the trailhead, that they had jogged much of the way, and that the last half mile of trail had been mighty dark. Caley called Sheridan and reported that the subjects made it out oky.

Analysis

The climbers were unhurt when they called 911. There has been a great deal of discussion about what is appropriate use of cell phones to call for help from the backcountry. If these climbers had not had a radio or cell phone, they probably would have wandered around and eventually found their way down. There is a chance that they could have gotten hypothermic, or slipped when trying to navigate steep terrain, so the call may have avoided an accident. Also, the "rescue" was executed by a single person, from the comfort of his office. However, getting off route is a condition that has happened to every mountaineer who has a reasonable amount of experience. If one is not willing or able to solve route finding problems, one should not put oneself in situations where route finding is needed. (Source: Dave Rusho, Seattle Mountain Rescue)

FALL ON ROCK, UNROPED, POSSIBLY OFF ROUTE
Washington, Guye Peak

On October 13, Ken Colburn (49) was climbing Guye Peak with a friend when he fell 300 feet over a cliff to his death. The two had just unroped near the summit when they reached easier terrain after climbing the west face. Ken was traversing across moss-covered wet rocks above the 300-foot cliff when he apparently tripped or slipped about 30 feet from the edge of the cliff. His friend was ahead when he saw Ken fall and try to grab some scrub alpine trees, but his fall and acceleration were so quick that he was unable to stop himself from going over the edge of the cliff. Rescuers later found Ken's hat at the location where he fell some 30 feet above the cliff. The body was recovered by helicopter the next day.

Analysis

In one 50-meter section, the normal scramble/descent route drops down the north side of the ridge, to avoid a steep, exposed section of rock. Ken fell to the south side of the ridge, from approximately the location of this steep area. He appears to have been off route. This is common route finding error of this peak. Believing he was on a scramble route may have led Ken to continue without a belay even though he was on exposed, technical ground. (Source: Dave Rusho, Seattle Mountain Rescue)

(Editor's Note: There were five climbing incident reports from Mount Rainier this year—in addition to the heart attack report. Two were overdue parties who returned without injury. One case involved a climber being hit in the abdomen by a "football sized" rock while ascending above Disappointment Cleaver. While the climber was able to descend on his own with his partner, it is worthwhile to note that the rock had been dislodged by a guided party above and they did not shout a warning.

Another incident involved a party of three who called for help when they experienced AMS and dehydration at the top of Disappointment Cleaver. After rehydration, rangers escorted them on the descent to Camp Muir.

The fifth incident involved two parties of two being struck by an avalanche at 13,500 feet on the Liberty Ridge Route in May. A helicopter evacuation was required.)

FALL ON ROCK, INADEQUATE PROTECTION
Wisconsin, Devil's Lake State Park

Two climbers (who are guides) were setting up individual top-ropes when John (21) heard the sound of a falling backpack. John called out to Elaine (20) and received no response. Knowing immediately the gravity of the situation, John placed the clients in a safe position and ran to the aid of Elaine.

Elaine had attached herself to a large but loose block with a #3 Camp Tri-Cam and a 20-foot section of one-inch tubular webbing. She had hopped over the edge of the cliff to a ledge five feet below to gain access to a crack to place protection for anchoring the top rope. As she leaned over the edge of this lower ledge to gain access to the crack, she felt a "pop" and fell over the edge. She fell 50 feet, hitting several large tree limbs and finally ending up on the mud and scree slope below.

John, who had Wilderness First Responder training, did immediate spine immobilization and checked her airway for breathing as he thought that she had not been breathing for those few minutes. She let out a large gasp of air and was very incoherent in verbal response. John sent his two eldest clients down to seek Ranger and rescue assistance.

Within 20 minutes, a rescue team arrived. Elaine was raised and prepped for a Flight For Life flight to Madison for her injuries. Elaine sustained a separated shoulder with fractures, a punctured lung, and a leg laceration. She was hospitalized for six days, three in intensive care and three for rehabilitation, after which she was released for home care. She admits to not using enough protection and credits her helmet for limiting injuries.

Analysis

Using proper and sufficient equipment is highly recommended. In this case, Elaine used only one piece of protection and attached it to a loose boulder. Perhaps she hadn't placed the protection adequately to prevent a side-loading that may have been put on the piece.

John was happy with his first aid training and stated, "The whole book just flashed before me," and was glad to be able to help. Whatever mistake was made, Elaine admits to not using enough protection. She is climbing and guiding again, but never gets near the edge unsecured and unroped. (Source: Steven Schaefgen)

FATIGUE—FALL ON ROCK, FAILURE TO FOLLOW ROUTE, EXCEEDING ABILITIES
Wisconsin, Devil's Lake State Park, Chicago

Two male climbers (ages unknown) were leading Chicago (5.9) at Devil's Lake State Park. "Josh" climbed the crux of the route but soon after got lost. He spent some time searching for the proper route, and after time his strength diminished and he fell. The only protection on the route was below the crux and the first ten to 15 feet above it was unprotected. Josh had placed a #4 Camalot and a CCH Alien below the crux, and as he fell the Camalot pulled from the route, lengthening the fall.

"John," below on belay, was approximately 20-30 pounds lighter than Josh. John had been sitting against a tree but was not anchored. As Josh fell, it pulled John from the tree and up to the first, and only, piece of protection about ten feet off the ground.

Thanks to the only piece of protection on the route, Josh stopped short of a full-fledged fall onto sharp pointed rocks. However, it did not stop him from partially hitting these rocks, causing minor injury to his legs, an arm laceration requiring eight stitches, and back pain that left him bearing a large "lump" or welt. They stopped climbing for the day and were both fortunate that injuries were minor.

Analysis
Both climbers are reported to be experienced and had climbed with each other often. It is also reported that both had just returned from a climbing trip out West. It has been mentioned that they may have been feeling "cocky" from success on western granite and misjudged their abilities on Devil's Lake quartzite, which is notorious for being "slippery" and can be inherently more difficult than granite due to that fact. The guidebook describes Chicago as "...a bold and heroic lead with serious potential ground fall." Unfortunately, Josh found that out first hand. Had it not been for the Alien holding the fall, Josh would have hit the pointed rocks at full force from his estimated height of 40 feet.

These two seemed to have overlooked the weight difference between them. In a top-rope situation there may be no danger if one climber is slightly heavier or lighter than the other, but it is a definite concern when leading. Either way, the belayer should always anchor in. (Source: Steven Schaefgen)

FALL ON ROCK, FAILURE TO FOLLOW ROUTE, PROTECTION PULLED OUT, INEXPERIENCE
Wisconsin, Devil's Lake State Park, Resurrection
A climber set out to do a classic route—Resurrection (5.9). Tom was a competent gym climber at 5.10+, but he had no experience leading on rock or placing protection.

Tom had problems finding the route and quickly lost his way and found that it was beyond his lead ability. After route searching for some time, Tom fell. As he fell, his protection, inadequately placed, pulled from the rock, and Tom sustained a 30-foot fall to the ground.

Luckily, there was a doctor nearby who stabilized Tom. Climbers were then sent to get help from park rangers, who arrived in the wrong area, as they had been misinformed by the climbers. The doctor and several climbers had already raised Tom from where he had fallen, so time had been wasted in arrival at the wrong location. The extent of injuries is unknown, but Tom was taken via ambulance to a nearby hospital for treatment.
Analysis
Assuming that climbing in a real rock environment is remotely related to gym climbing can be very costly. (Source: Steven Schaefgen)

(Editor's Note: We are pleased to have a new correspondent from this part of the climbing world—Steven Schaefgen—who also offered the following:

It should also be stressed that there are many accidents every year at Devil's Lake State Park, Wisconsin. However, most of the accidents that happen on or around the rock bluffs and cliffs are non-climbing related and do not involve climbers. The bluffs at Devil's Lake State Park are accessible via many trails and offer exposed views of the lake and surrounding area. Unfortunately, many visitors are injured every year by getting too close, "messing around," and scrambling around boulders and bluffs. People usually get hurt because they get into a climbing situation without experience.

There were many cases of broken bones, lacerations, and head injuries not involving climbers. One death occurred last year at Devil's Lake State Park. A man was jumping back and forth between two bluffs, stumbled, and fell 80 feet to his death.

It was reported that there was a non-climbing death at Gibraltar Rock State Park as well. Gibraltar Rock State Park is currently closed for climbing, but hikers and sight-seers are permitted. Gibraltar Rock offers bluffs with heights over 100 feet. The report was that a person was standing too close to the edge, turned, slipped on dirt, and fell some 100 feet to his death, hitting several trees on the way down.)

FALL ON ROCK, INADEQUATE PROTECTION
West Virginia, Seneca Rocks, Triple Si

Regrettably I must report my involvement in another climbing accident. I was leading Triple Si, a dihedral climb on August 10. About ten feet from the top, I was having trouble figuring out a crux move and decided to put in a stopper at the crux, even though I had a solid cam about three feet below the crux. The stopper jammed before it was set well. I knew this and tested it with body weight, and then ignored it as I had the cam below. I re-climbed the crux and still didn't see the combination. On down-climbing I fell, and the stopper pulled. My fall was only ten feet, but at nine feet I landed full force with my right foot on a chock stone in the crack. The result was a ruptured Achilles tendon. The injury (and complications) has cost more than $50,000 and six months to a year of climbing.

Analysis

The lesson: Take time to place good protection and check the fall potential, particularly at cruxes.

One last comment: It certainly pays to climb with a partner trained in rescue and Wilderness First Aid. Carole Simmons lowered me, bandaged my foot, hiked my pack down the mountain, brought up Leki poles, and got me down the trail. Thanks, Carole.

P.S. As owner and President of The Challenge Rock Climbing School based in Atlanta, GA, I use every accident or incident as a learning experience. Our general analysis covers three parts: One, What happened? Two, What was done that led to the accident? And three, What wasn't done that could have prevented the accident? Every year I note and copy for our instructors and climbing partners portions of your Accident Report. Thanks for your good work. (Source: Jerry Dodgen, Professional Member of AMGA, Member of AAC Since 1989)

(Editor's Note: Here is a letter that Jerry sent forward to the leading staff of the school.

CLIMBERS! Accidents happen! We know that, and we try to prevent them. Prevention of accidents in rock climbing is critical because they can result in serious injury, or death. We know that too on an intellectual level. Well, I know it on a painfully personal level. On my accident August 2001, I fell only ten feet but at nine feet my right foot hit a chock stone—with enough force to completely rupture my Achilles tendon.

This accident could have been prevented had I taken three minutes to reset a stopper that was poorly set at the crux. Since I had a bomber cam three feet below the stopper I didn't consider it much, but when it pulled it allowed me an extra 6 feet of fall. Sitting around for a month with my foot in the air allowed me to realize how often I have let poor placements slide because I didn't think I would fall. It's kind of stupid to place a piece of protection that won't catch you just because you don't think you will fall. By that thinking I might as well free-solo. I learned two things. One, place solid pro, and two, check the potential fall, particularly at a crux. I knew these things intellectually, but the pain, cost, and inconvenience and out of commission time has me really knowing them now.

All accidents are learning opportunities. Read (no Study!) the following excerpts from *Accidents in North American Mountaineering*. They deal with common incidents that we experience almost every time we're on the rock. Note how many times a minor decision or small incident led to grave consequences.

I understand more fully what Kathryn has always said: that anything happening should be considered a "mishap or accident," something to train us. Right down to many scrapes and rock rash on "My First Time Rock Climbing Trips" can indicate something more serious about to happen... Get a low-cost lesson!

Also, on another matter, we have the following from Steve Pack about a report in ANAM 2001, *pages 82-83: "One particular error sticks out in the accident description for Seneca Rocks. It lists it as being in VIRGINIA. The last time I checked, unless they moved it, Seneca Rocks is in WEST VIRGINIA, a completely different state since 1863! There is even an editors note... This is a bit of a sore point with me, since I still run into people who are incredulous when I tell them West Virginia is a separate state from Virginia." Apologies, especially to Steve, as he is a West Virginia native.)*

OUT OF BOUNDS—LOST, INADEQUATE CLOTHING AND EQUIPMENT
Wyoming, Grand Teton National Park, Rock Spring Canyon
On February 6 at 1330, Cameron Morgan (25), Jonathan Gagne (25), and Katherine Gagne (24) left the Teton Village Ski Area boundaries with the intent to ski out of bounds in Rock Springs Canyon. They were on alpine skis and a snowboard. The avalanche danger was listed as "Considerable." They took a wrong turn and entered Granite Canyon in Grand Teton National Park and headed north, not south. They were unable to retrace their tracks and spent the night at the bottom of the canyon. On the following afternoon, a fourth member of the group reported that his companions had not returned.

Grand Teton National Park rangers were notified by the ski patrol at about 1430. Rangers and a ski patrolman were flown by helicopter to search the Granite Canyon area and located the missing party from the air. They were picked up just before nightfall and flown from the backcountry. Despite the ordeal, all three members of the party were in good condition and were released.
Analysis
Aside from the clothes they were wearing and a Camelback with water, they had no other survival gear, such as food, extra clothing, matches, shovel, probes,

or transceivers. They did have a Teton Village ski area map in their possession. They were sure that they were skiing through Rock Springs Canyon to the south of Teton Village, as they had done previously. When they reached Granite Creek, the water was flowing the wrong way. When skiing out of Rock Springs, one has to turn left to get back to the ski area. The stream was flowing to their right. Assuming that the water wasn't really flowing downhill, they went upstream to where they spent the night. The next morning their discussions about the direction of the water continued. Interesting group dynamics undoubtedly took place. Leadership was asserted, and the party spent the day going about a quarter-mile further upstream before they were spotted from the helicopter.

Leadership skills and backcountry survival preparedness are just as important when accessing the wilderness from a developed ski area as they are when heading into the wilderness with a mind-set of seeking a wilderness experience. A second night out in –20 degrees F. in their condition might have been grim.

Another factor was the reporting party. He assumed that they didn't meet apres-ski in the bar and that they didn't get back to the motel that night "because they were partying." He searched the lifts at the ski area the following day until 1430 before reporting the party overdue. (Source: Dan Burgette, SAR Ranger, Grand Teton National Park)

(Editor's Note: While this is not a climbing incident, it is included as a classic example of a backcountry situation that required mountaineering skills for which the participants were not prepared.)

OFF ROUTE—UNFAMILIAR WITH DESCENT, WEATHER
Wyoming, Grand Teton National Park, Grand Teton

On June 11 around 0100, Swis Stockton and Michael Feldman left the Lupine Meadows trailhead with the intention of climbing the Exum Ridge on the Grand Teton in a one-day effort in an attempt to beat a predicted storm. They had just arrived in Jackson Hole from the east coast and left at 0100 after an hour's sleep. They moved slower than expected and discussed turning around at the Lower Saddle and again at Wallstreet—but didn't. They started their descent of the Owen-Spalding Route from the top of the Open Book pitch in the last of the daylight. As they began the rappels, a severe storm engulfed them. With high winds, blowing snow, and limited visibility, at 0100 hours they decided to bivouac for the night in snow caves in the Wall Street Gully. They started moving at 0500 and assumed they were not on the standard descent. They went back to the Upper Saddle and started following cairns until they became cliffed-out. They went back to the Upper Saddle to get reoriented and started down the Idaho Express gully. They reached a drop-off with a rappel station and realized that they were disoriented. They started to climb back to the Upper Saddle, the last point on the mountain they were sure of. If they couldn't find the right descent route, they intended to start rappelling.

Stockton and Feldman had left gear in their cabin at the AAC Climbers Ranch. This was reported to Grand Teton National Park by another person who was lodging there on the morning of June 12. The weather was deteriorating, with a low cloud cover. The park contract helicopter was able to fly seven park rangers to the Lower Saddle on the Grand Teton before conditions worsened. Six of the rangers began a search of the Owen-Spalding route. At 1409, Rangers McConnell and Jackson made contact with Stockton and Feldman as they climbed toward the Upper Saddle. They were in good condition. Stockton and Feldman were assisted to the Lower Saddle, where their condition was assessed. They were able to descend to the valley by themselves. The rescue team also descended, reaching the trailhead at about 2000.

Analysis

Stockton and Feldman felt they were in control of their situation. They had heard the helicopter, but they didn't think it was associated with them. They didn't want to follow the rangers because they had already gone down that way, and it didn't work. This party had good gear and extra food. They didn't feel there was any reason to get excited over their late return.

It's important to realize that when a party doesn't return when there is severe weather in the mountains, people worry about the party's safety. When the rescue team is called, we are obligated to investigate. In this case, a call to the Exum guides on the Lower Saddle said that the mountain was in bad condition, and they had to turn back that morning. Past parties caught out in storms with snow and high winds have shown us that there is cause for concern. That is the reason that we accepted the costs and risks of flying to the Lower Saddle and searching in marginal conditions. Sometimes conditions in the mountains are the reason we should do a rock climb down low. Sometimes it's our physical limitations due to lack of acclimatization or our need for rest that should cause us to choose less-ambitious goals. Setting out on a major undertaking like a day climb of the Grand Teton when not at the top of your game, especially knowing that a storm cycle is predicted, should result in being more conservative. When the party is not progressing as rapidly as anticipated, there is good cause to lower the goals or turn around. (Source: Dan Burgette, SAR Ranger, Grand Teton National Park)

FALLING ROCK—FALL ON ROCK, IMPROPER BELAY TECHNIQUE, INADEQUATE PROTECTION
Wyoming, Grand Teton National Park, Nez Perce

On June 30 about 9:30 a.m., Jeff Heinrichs (29) of Jackson, WY, took a leader fall on Nez Perce. He was unable to walk after the fall, so his partner, Dave Simpson (33), went for help.

Heinrichs was leading the first pitch of what he thought was the South Ridge of Nez Perce, but in fact he was east of the normal route. He was trying to place his first piece of protection about thirty feet above the talus. His belayer, using an ATC, wasn't anchored as he sat on a ledge about fifteen feet beneath the leader. A large block that Heinrichs was standing on fell away, so he fell about thirty feet before hitting the talus. Simpson instinctively reached for the rope and began to haul in slack. He was unable to hold the fall, and as the rope slipped through his hands, they were burned. Heinrichs continued to tumble down the slope for another fifty feet. His helmet and pack saved him from serious injury.

Analysis

The lack of an anchor and proper belaying technique resulted in an eighty foot fall instead of a thirty-footer. Fortunately the belayer wasn't pulled from his ledge. (Source: Dan Burgette, SAR Ranger, Grand Teton National Park)

RAPPEL ERROR—NO BACK-UP ON RAPPEL, FALL ON ROCK, BEING IN A HURRY

Wyoming, Grand Teton National Park, Grand Teton, Owen-Spalding

On July 18, Ryan Sasser (27) and I, Holly Beck (26), got a late start out of our Moraine Camp on the Grand Teton due to an early morning rainstorm. Hiking up to the Lower Saddle, we reached the base of the Petzoldt Ridge around 8:00 a.m. We topped out on the Petzoldt Ridge before noon and continued to the Upper Exum Ridge to complete our route. We had climbed the entire Petzoldt Ridge in coats and gloves, and by the time we started up the Exum Ridge, we were climbing in intermittent snow and rain. At the bottom of the Windtunnel pitch we had to hide out for about twenty minutes while a brief hailstorm beat down. We finally summited just after 3:00 p.m. We had seen parties on the Upper Exum that day, so we were surprised to have the summit to ourselves. We had brought a topo and a photo of the Owen-Spalding route for the descent. It was clear that a storm was coming in when we headed down.

On our way down we were never really sure if we were actually following the "official" descent route. When we got to a spot that looked like an anchor for a big rappel on the often-guided climb we decided that was our rappel to the Upper Saddle. Ryan rigged the rappel, tied knots in the end of the rope and tossed the rope straight down. We could see that the rope was not touching the ground, but we had been told by more than one climber to expect this and that we would only reach the ground with rope stretch. Even though Ryan weighs more than I, we decided that I should go down first since I was a more experienced climber. I felt that if we had to do a second rappel, I would be able to set it up more easily. I took some gear with me in case I needed it and went down the rope. I chose to rappel without an auto-block, since I rarely use this type of backup.

The farther I got on rappel the more I could see that I was not going to get to the ground. Since this was a free-hanging rappel, I was kicking against the wall to keep myself moving and my options open. Looking around, I spotted a ledge to the left that I thought I could drop onto from above. I planned to get a handhold with my left hand and get my feet on the wall, and then downclimb or drop onto the ledge. In order to make it to the ledge, I decided to untie the knots in my rope to prevent them from becoming stuck in my belay device before I reached the ledge. With this plan in mind, I untied the knots and started kicking towards the wall above the ledge. I found a handhold with my left hand that felt promising. On my next swing in I grabbed it again just to see if it was good. As I did so, I lost control of my brake hand, probably as my left hand was holding me in to the wall but my momentum was swinging me back to the right.

As I was falling, I felt my helmet hit the rock several times before I crashed to the ground. I lay there for a few moments wondering if I didn't hurt too badly yet just because I was in shock. I had fallen about twenty feet. I sat up and tried to assess my condition. My arm hurt and I felt moisture in my sleeve. I managed to get my shell off and saw blood on my left arm coming through my fleece shirt. Within a couple minutes Ryan was on rappel. I yelled to him in mid-rappel that I had fallen. He made the jump to the ledge and came to check me out. Based on the amount of pain I was in and the obvious trauma to my arm, Ryan was concerned about the possibility of fractures. He moved me to a somewhat sheltered spot and went for help. Three hours later, Exum guide David Bowers reached me, having hiked up from the Lower Saddle, and started administering first aid. He was followed closely behind by Ranger Scott Gunther, who had been flown to the scene, and fellow Exum Guides Pete Delannoy and Miles Smart. The plan was to take me out by helicopter if possible. However, just as help reached the scene, the storm started and it was not safe for the helicopter to be so close to the Upper Saddle.

Instead, we hiked and scrambled down to the Lower Saddle in intense whiteout conditions complete with lightening. Members of the party at times could feel strike, although no one was hit. It took us about two hours to reach the Lower Saddle with Scott and David navigating the way down and me moving mostly on my own power, but helped by a short-rope through the scrambling sections. We were greeted with more help at the Eye of the Needle and made it safely back to the huts at the Lower Saddle.

I received amazing medical care there under the supervision of Rangers Dan Burgette and Ron Johnson. Ranger Craig Holm watched over me all night long. In the morning I was evacuated by helicopter to St. John's Hospital where I underwent surgery to clean and close the large wound I had received in my arm. Luckily I had avoided injuring any muscles or nerves and had not broken any bones. The doctors were amazed at the quality of care I had received on the mountain, calling it real hospital care.

I was able to start climbing again in just a few weeks, although it took a couple of outings to be ready to lead and rappel again. Within two months I was fully recovered and back climbing at Smith Rock and in Yosemite. I am so grateful for the quick response and amazing care I received from my rescuers. This could have easily have been a more serious accident and I feel fortunate to have recovered from it so quickly and easily.

Analysis

I believe the biggest contributing factor to this accident was being in a hurry. I was tired from the climb and nervous about the storm coming in. Mentally I was focused just on getting off the rock as fast as possible. This led me to take a chance on swinging onto the ledge without any backup, or without considering other options like ascending the ropes and re-rigging the rappel. As it turns out, we were rappelling in the correct location, but needed to throw the rope to the left in order to reach higher ground. In this situation I took a chance that ended up working for my partner but not for me. (Source: Holly Beck)

FAILURE TO TEST HOLD—HAND-HOLD CAME OFF, FALL ON ROCK
Wyoming, Grand Teton National Park, Grand Teton, Petzoldt Ridge

On July 20, Ben Wessler (20) was leading the pitch above the Window on the Petzoldt Ridge of the Grand Teton. He placed a piece of protection with a long sling about eight feet above the belay ledge. About four feet above the piece, he tested a large rock feature about the size of a basketball. He grabbed the feature with both hands and it pulled loose when he weighted it. He hit the belay ledge with his left foot and butt as the rope came tight. He stopped on the eight-foot wide ledge. His partner, Tim McMahill and three of their companions climbing with them on a separate rope, helped Ben rappel the steep places and lower him down less-steep places. When they reached easier ground, Ben's brother Matt went on ahead to seek help at the Exum hut. The remaining climbers lowered Ben two more rope lengths to the base of the ridge at about 12,000 feet.

Exum guide Bill McKenna reported the injury to Teton Dispatch by cell phone just after 1800. A park contract helicopter piloted by Rick Harmon ferried five rangers to the Lower Saddle. With the help of three guides, the rangers splinted the leg and carried Ben to the heli-spot on the Lower Saddle. He was flown to Lupine Meadows at 2050. Medic I transported him to St. John's Hospital in Jackson. Two pins were placed in his foot to stabilize the fracture.

Analysis

This incident involved a large feature that was from all indications part of the mountain before it broke. Testing holds, even big ones, is advisable, especially when unroped. This incident was a good example of good belaying, first aid, self-rescue, and responsibility in the mountains. (Source: Dan Burgette, SAR Ranger, Grand Teton National Park)

HANDHOLD CAME OFF—FALL ON ROCK
Wyoming, Grand Teton National Park, Symmetry Spire

On July 28, Laura Plaut (35) was treated and evacuated from near the summit of 10,546-foot Symmetry Spire after she fell about 100 feet, shattering her left elbow and breaking a bone in her left foot. Plaut and her climbing partner sought out a hiker with a cell phone and called rangers for help about 4:30 p.m. Using the Park's contract helicopter, the first of the rescue team was able to make his way to Plaut's side by shortly after 6:15 p.m. and provided initial treatment. At that time, a determination was made to evacuate Plaut from the mountainside with the use of a litter suspended below the helicopter. She was subsequently transported to St. John's Hospital in Jackson by park ambulance.

Analysis

Plaut's climbing partner told Park Rangers that they had just completed ascending the Southwest Ridge route of Symmetry Spire and were headed for the summit when the accident occurred. Plaut was scrambling unroped (not an uncommon occurrence on this scramble) near the summit of the spire when she apparently grabbed a loose rock and fell. Her partner said he could see that Plaut had an open fracture of her elbow, a hurt ankle, and a head laceration and was concerned about the possibility of other injuries, and so he immediately sought help. She was wearing a helmet. (Source: Dan Burgette, SAR Ranger, Grand Teton National Park)

FALL ON ROCK
Wyoming, Grand Teton National Park, Table Mountain

On August 8, Don Rassler reported that his climbing partner, Ben Goodwin (22), had fallen about 10-20 feet while down-climbing the first pitch of Heartbreak Ridge on Table Mountain around 0830. He barely began to catch Goodwin on the climbing rope when Goodwin landed squarely on his back near him. Being in a precarious location, the two were able to down-climb a short distance to a safe location, at which time Rassler, a Wilderness First Responder, decided to seek rescue assistance due to what he felt was significant injury to Goodwin's lower back, with potential spinal compromise.

Ranger Johnson received the initial report and relayed information to rescue coordinator Montopoli. The contract helicopter transported seven rangers to a landing zone in the South Fork of Cascade Canyon near the injured climber. Rangers Burgette, Guenther, and Johnson climbed to Goodwin, rendered medical assistance, and after evaluating the scene determined that a short-haul operation was the best method of extraction. Medical control was contacted and concurred with the decision.

Goodwin was short-hauled to the landing zone. Goodwin was then flown internally to Lupine Meadows with Rangers Perch and Jernigan as attendants. Goodwin was then transferred to the park ambulance and transported to St. John's Hospital. He was treated for abrasions and contusions and released. He had no spinal injury.

Analysis

Having medical training is important for climbers. Rassler did a good job of assessing that there might be a significant spinal injury due to the mechanism of injury and the signs and symptoms. The contusions Goodwin received to his back resulted in pain that could have been associated with a spinal injury. Without an X-ray machine, everyone treated Goodwin as if he had a spinal injury. A basic knowledge of what to do and what NOT to do can make a big difference when a member of your party is hurt. (Source: Dan Burgette, SAR Ranger, Grand Teton National Park)

FAILURE TO TEST HOLDS—HANDHOLD CAME OFF, FALL ON ROCK
Wyoming, Wind River Range, Jackson Peak

On August 11 about 1100, Bev Boynton (51) and David Moore of Jackson, WY, were finishing the final pitch on the South Buttress of Jackson Peak in the Wind River Range of Wyoming. While Boynton was leading at about 12,800 feet, she pulled off a large flake of rock which caused her to fall about fifteen feet onto the ledge below. She sustained multiple injuries and believed that she had a pneumothorax. Moore gave her warm clothes and went for assistance. When he arrived at Indian Basin, he located campers with a cell phone and called the Jenny Lake Ranger Station in Grand Teton National Park. When the Sublette County Sheriff's Office was notified, they requested the park rangers assist in the rescue.

Two park rangers and a Physician's Assistant were flown to Moore's location in Indian Basin. Helicopter short-haul technique was then used to insert rescuers to the accident site. Boynton's injuries were assessed and treated, and she was short-hauled to the basin below. Boynton was then transferred to an air ambulance from the Eastern Idaho Regional Medical Center and flown to St. John's Hospital in Jackson. She had multiple injuries, including a pulmonary contusion and torn ankle ligaments.

Analysis

This is another case of a large block pulling loose. A very experienced climber was caught by this objective danger. Testing holds and not having the belayer standing directly below the climber are important. This was a good example of climbers with a different mind-set than we often see in the Tetons. This party was nineteen miles from the trailhead. Boynton assumed that she would be spending the night on her ledge, and the party was prepared for that, mentally and gear-wise. Amazingly, the cell phone Moore borrowed got out of the basin beneath the peak and Boynton was evacuated that evening. Cell phones can be a real help when they are genuinely needed and if they work, but they are not more important than self-help and being prepared. (Source: Dan Burgette, SAR Ranger, Grand Teton National Park)

HANDHOLD CAME OFF—STRUCK BY ROCK
Wyoming, Grand Teton National Park, Disappointment Peak

On August 17, John Taylor (29) was climbing the Lake Ledges route on Disappointment Peak when he dislodged a rock. The rock struck him on the left chest, and then hit his feet and ankles. He tumbled about ten feet after the rock passed. His sister ran down for help. Ranger Andy Byerly saw her run past him, but thought she was just a jogger. Another visitor informed Byerly of the incident. He radioed the information he had at 1630 to SAR coordinator Burgette. Rangers Jackson and Motter had just finished the Open Book climb on the south side of Disappointment, and they were only about 200 yards from Taylor when they heard Byerly's report. Climbing with them was Dr. Oram, an emergency physician. They reached Taylor, did an assessment, and requested that a helicopter be dispatched. After discussion, it was decided to fly to the scene, do a power check, and if everything looked good, land on the plateau above the incident site, let out ranger Johnson with med gear, and return for the short-haul litter.

The park's contract helicopter, piloted by Jim Hood, arrived at the SAR cache at 1712. After a briefing, they flew to the site and found good conditions. The patient was packaged and short-hauled to the heli-spot, and then flown inside the ship to Lupine Meadows where Medic I was waiting to transport Taylor to St. John's Hospital. The rescue team was flown from the heli-spot and reached Lupine Meadows at 1910.

Taylor was found to have lacerations, contusions, and fractures in his left foot.

Analysis
This was one example of a climber being caught unaware as a loose rock pulled free of the mountain. Testing holds when scrambling unroped is just as important as when on lead. (Source: Dan Burgette, SAR Ranger, Grand Teton National Park)

BELAY ANCHOR FAILURE—KNOT CAME UNDONE, FALL ON ROCK
Wyoming, Grand Teton National Park, Mount Owen
On the evening of September 3, a cell phone call reported an Exum client with a sprained ankle on the West Ledges of Mount Owen. Tanya Bradby of Seattle, WA, was on a guided climb of the Grand Traverse. After spending the night of September 2 on the east ridge of Mount Owen, they went to the summit and started descending the West Ledges. About three hundred feet below the crest of the south ridge, they came to a steep step of ten or more feet. The guide decided to lower the client down this step. Earlier, the guide had threaded an anchor with a sling. After using the thread, she didn't retie the knot on the sling. For the lowering, she took the sling she had threaded before, tied a knot to join its ends, and slung a boulder. She clipped a locking carabiner into the sling and used a Munter hitch. As Bradby weighted the rope, the sling failed because the knot came undone. Bradby got her foot stuck in a crack during her fall, and her ankle was sprained as a result. Bradby hit a ledge below the step, and the guide was able to hang onto the 8-mm rope with her burned hands, which kept Bradby from tumbling down the seventy-degree face.

Analysis
This is a sobering incident. An experienced guide tied a knot that failed when it was weighted. This reaffirms the basic rule that one has to check and recheck all knots and anchors before a life is trusted to them. This incident should get the attention of all, including experienced climbers. (Source: Dan Burgette, SAR Ranger, Grand Teton National Park)

(Editor's Note: As Peter Lev, one of Exum Guides owners pointed out, "...these things have happened to just about every climber at one time or another; but what really matters is that the guide SAVED THE DAY by hand holding a small-diameter rope. No small feat. It is the 'save' that separates out the climbers/guides with 'the right stuff.'")

ROCK PULLED OFF—BROKE CLIMBING ROPE, FALL ON ROCK
Wyoming, Wind River Range, Cirque of the Towers, Wolf's Head Peak
On September 22, Michael "Scott" Shaw (31) of Talkeetna, Alaska, died in a mountaineering accident while descending Wolf's Head Peak in the Cirque of the Towers.

Scott and Alex Everett (both National Outdoor Leadership School instructors) summited Wolf's Head Peak via the East Ridge around 4:10 p.m. They rappelled the west face by double rope rappel then climbed 4th class to the notch above a prominent east facing chimney/gully descending to Cirque Lake. They made four single rope rappels to the floor of the gully. On the fourth and last rappel, the rappel rope became stuck when they tried to retrieve it. They decided that Scott would climb back up to dislodge it. Scott climbed, belayed by

Alex. He placed four pieces of protection and was about 60 feet up when Alex heard Scott yell, "ROCK!" When Alex looked up, he saw Scott and a rock about the size of a tire—and estimated to be about 250 pounds—falling. Alex braced for a hard pull on the rope, but it never came. He saw Scott hit a ledge above him, then bounce and tumble down the gully approximately 250-300 feet.

Alex descended to Scott and administered first aid and CPR. By 7:10—after about 25 minutes—Scott did not respond to CPR. Alex covered Scott and descended to the valley and found another climbing party. With one person from that party Alex hiked out to Big Sandy Opening, and they drove to Lander. They called the NOLS Alaska branch school (the only phone number Alex had with him) and reached Kurt Gisclair. Kurt then called the Fremont County Sheriff.

On September 23, the Fremont County Search and Rescue group organized a response using climbing rangers from Grand Teton National Park. Alex and the county coroner were flown to the site, and the climbing rangers investigated the accident. Alex and the coroner returned to Lander.

Analysis

Based on this investigation, it appears that Scott pulled the rock off, which then pinched and cut his climbing rope against another rock. Scott was found with about two feet of rope still tied to his harness. (Source: Drew Leemon and Alex Everett)

HAPE, HACE, AND AMS
Wyoming, Grand Teton National Park

While signs and symptoms of AMS are not unusual in the Tetons, it is rare to see HAPE or HACE. During the summer of 2001, four significant altitude-related cases were seen. One was a 14 year old boy scout from Sugar City, ID, who had climbed the Middle and South Tetons from the South Fork of Cascade Canyon on July 24. At 1900, Ranger Jim Springer encountered the group at their campsite in the South Fork. The scout was complaining of headache, nausea, ataxia, and chest pain. Springer was able to hear gurgling in the boy's chest and surmised that it was HAPE. Springer hiked the boy to lower elevation, and his condition improved as they got lower. They spent the night at the patrol cabin at 8,500 feet, and the gurgling was absent at that elevation.

Two brothers, Mike (24) and Joe (19) Baker, flew in from Pennsylvania on August 17 and immediately set out for a day climb of the Grand Teton. Rangers Jernigan, McConnell, and Vidak were told by a guide that two climbers were having difficulty. One had vomited above the rappel, and they appeared weak. The rangers found the brothers at the Upper Saddle. Joe was curled up on the ground with headache and other AMS symptoms. Mike seemed in worse shape with nausea and weakness. They were escorted to the Lower Saddle where their blood pressures were found to be low. Joe improved with lower elevation, food, and rest. After contacting medical control, Mike was administered two liters of I.V. fluids. Their condition improved enough to hike them out to the trailhead.

Caltha Crowe (54) and her husband from Connecticut were backpacking into Hanging Canyon, also on August 17, when she began projectile vomiting. Her husband thought her problem was overheating, so he sat her in the creek. Rangers Jernigan and Larson were flown to their location and felt that the woman should be rapidly evacuated. She was flown with Jernigan to Lupine Meadows, where she was transferred into an ambulance. On the way to town, her condition rapidly deteriorated. She nearly died in the ER. She was diagnosed with HAPE. Her treatment was complicated by the hypothermia resulting from sitting in the stream.

On September 4, Seth Uptain (24) and Todd Lamppa (28) from Casper, WY, set out to attempt a "light and fast" ascent of the East Ridge of the Grand Teton. They camped the night of September 2 at Surprise Lake and began climbing early the next morning. By 1800, they had reached the upper part of the mountain above the Second Tower at about 13,100 feet. Uptain began feeling increasingly ill with a terrible headache and difficulty breathing. They decided to stop for the night since Uptain was having trouble with balance as well as gaining altitude. They set up their tent. Uptain's condition worsened during the night, and at 0430, Lamppa called park Dispatch with a cell phone to report that Uptain couldn't stand and that his lungs gurgled noticeably.

Rangers Bywater and Johnson set out from the Lower Saddle with med gear and arrived at 0740. Uptain reported that he had HAPE the previous winter on a ski trip to 11,000 feet. His lungs were wet, but there was no gurgling heard without a stethoscope. He was ataxic. A screamer suit ride to Lupine Meadows was conducted, since the winds at the Lower Saddle weren't good for landing there. When Uptain arrived at the ambulance, he couldn't stand, but he refused transport to the hospital since he didn't have health insurance and he had recovered after three days last winter. An I.V. was started, and he was convinced to go to the hospital. By the time he arrived at the ER, his gurgling chest was quite apparent. He again tried to deny treatment due to costs. After some treatment, he left the hospital.

Analysis

These cases show that it is possible to have serious altitude problems with moderate elevation gains if one is susceptible. They also should reinforce that climbers should listen to their bodies. It is better to go downhill if your condition is GOING downhill rather 0than pushing until you can't help yourself. At least two of these people would have died if others hadn't intervened and got them to help at lower elevation. It should also be obvious that climbers need to understand what "light and fast" means. As for health insurance and/or the cost of treatment, one must be aware of the consequences. (Source: Dan Burgette, SAR Ranger, Grand Teton National Park and Jed Williamson)

STATISTICAL TABLES

TABLE I
REPORTED MOUNTAINEERING ACCIDENTS

	Number of Accidents Reported		Total Persons Involved		Injured		Fatalities	
	USA	CAN	USA	CAN	USA	CAN	USA	CAN
1951	15		22		11		3	
1952	31		35		17		13	
1953	24		27		12		12	
1954	31		41		31		8	
1955	34		39		28		6	
1956	46		72		54		13	
1957	45		53		28		18	
1958	32		39		23		11	
1959	42	2	56	2	31	0	19	2
1960	47	4	64	12	37	8	19	4
1961	49	9	61	14	45	10	14	4
1962	71	1	90	1	64	0	19	1
1963	68	11	79	12	47	10	19	2
1964	53	11	65	16	44	10	14	3
1965	72	0	90	0	59	0	21	0
1966	67	7	80	9	52	6	16	3
1967	74	10	110	14	63	7	33	5
1968	70	13	87	19	43	12	27	5
1969	94	11	125	17	66	9	29	2
1970	129	11	174	11	88	5	15	5
1971	110	17	138	29	76	11	31	7
1972	141	29	184	42	98	17	49	13
1973	108	6	131	6	85	4	36	2
1974	96	7	177	50	75	1	26	5
1975	78	7	158	22	66	8	19	2
1976	137	16	303	31	210	9	53	6
1977	121	30	277	49	106	21	32	11
1978	118	17	221	19	85	6	42	10
1979	100	36	137	54	83	17	40	19
1980	191	29	295	85	124	26	33	8
1981	97	43	223	119	80	39	39	6
1982	140	48	305	126	120	43	24	14
1983	187	29	442	76	169	26	37	7
1984	182	26	459	63	174	15	26	6
1985	195	27	403	62	190	22	17	3
1986	203	31	406	80	182	25	37	14
1987	192	25	377	79	140	23	32	9
1988	156	18	288	44	155	18	24	4
1989	141	18	272	36	124	11	17	9
1990	136	25	245	50	125	24	24	4
1991	169	20	302	66	147	11	18	6
1992	175	17	351	45	144	11	43	6

	Number of Accidents Reported		Total Persons Involved		Injured		Fatalities	
	USA	CAN	USA	CAN	USA	CAN	USA	CAN
1993	132	27	274	50	121	17	21	1
1994	158	25	335	58	131	25	27	5
1995	168	24	353	50	134	18	37	7
1996	139	28	261	59	100	16	31	6
1997	158	35	323	87	148	24	31	13
1998	138	24	281	55	138	18	20	1
1999	123	29	248	69	91	20	17	10
2000	150	23	301	36	121	23	24	7
2001	150	22	276	47	138	14	16	2
TOTALS	5375	800	9805	1686	4590	636	1235	268

TABLE II

	1951–2000			2001		
Geographical Districts	Number of Accidents	Deaths	Total Persons Involved	Number of Accidents	Deaths	Total Persons Involved
Canada						
Alberta	431	126	942	18	2	40
British Columbia	273	106	608	3	0	5
Yukon Territory	33	26	73	0	0	0
Ontario	36	10	65	1	0	2
Quebec	30	7	63	0	0	0
East Arctic	7	2	20	0	0	0
West Arctic	1	1	2	0	0	0
Practice Cliffs[1]	20	2	36	0	0	0
United States						
Alaska	419	163	676	10	0	11
Arizona, Nevada Texas	76	15	142	2	1	3
Atlantic–North	84	103	332	34	1	57
Atlantic–South	80	23	1417	3	0	6
California	1093	244	2181	23	2	55
Central	127	15	204	4	1	7
Colorado	671	192	1167	20	1	42
Montana, Idaho South Dakota	75	30	118	0	0	0
Oregon	152	76	367	19	2	27
Utah, New Mexico	127	48	232	11	2	27
Washington	956	289	933	11	5	28
Wyoming	498	115	921	15	1	26

[1]This category includes bouldering, artificial climbing walls, buildings, and so forth. These are also added to the count of each province, but not to the total count, though that error has been made in previous years. The Practice Cliffs category has been removed from the U.S. data.

TABLE III

	1951–00 USA	1959–00 CAN.	2001 USA	2001 CAN.
Terrain				
Rock	3844	466	110	8
Snow	2199	330	31	5
Ice	211	118	11	9
River	13	3	0	0
Unknown	22	8	0	0
Ascent or Descent				
Ascent	2438	501	115	15
Descent	2080	342	32	5
Unknown	247	5	0	2
Other[N.B.]	0	0	5	0
Immediate Cause				
Fall or slip on rock	2678	253	90	3
Slip on snow or ice	874	178	17	6
Falling rock, ice, or object	537	122	18	3
Exceeding abilities	467	28	14	1
Avalanche	268	114	1	3
Exposure	243	13	2	0
Illness[1]	315	22	13	1
Stranded	288	40	8	2
Rappel Failure/Error[2]	237	41	9	2
Loss of control/glissade	182	16	1	0
Fall into crevasse/moat	145	44	3	2
Failure to follow route	142	28	9	1
Nut/chock pulled out	138	4	15	1
Piton/ice screw pulled out	87	12	0	0
Faulty use of crampons	78	5	4	0
Lightning	42	7	1	0
Skiing[3]	50	9	0	0
Ascending too fast	47	0	13	0
Equipment failure	11	2	1	0
Other[4]	301	32	13	0
Unknown	60	8	1	0
Contributory Causes				
Climbing unroped	934	155	7	2
Exceeding abilities	860	196	5	1
Inadequate equipment/clothing	586	75	21	3
Placed no/inadequate protection	570	84	30	2
Weather	409	58	11	2
Climbing alone	345	61	6	2
No hard hat	276	28	9	0
Nut/chock pulled out	194	17	2	0
Inadequate belay	152	24	15	1
Darkness	128	19	3	0
Poor position	135	18	0	2
Party separated	105	10	3	0
Piton/ice screw pulled out	85	11	0	1

	1951–00 USA	1959–00 CAN.	2001 USA	2001 CAN.
Contributory Causes, cont.				
Failure to test holds	81	22	6	2
Exposure	56	13	0	0
Failed to follow directions	69	11	0	0
Illness[1]	37	6	0	2
Equipment failure	11	7	0	0
Other[4]	243	91	1	5
Age of Individuals				
Under 15	118	12	3	0
15-20	1193	201	14	0
21-25	1225	238	42	0
26-30	1115	200	22	1
31-35	761	107	16	0
36-50	981	131	29	0
Over 50	162	23	9	1
Unknown	1043	629	45	45
Experience Level				
None/Little	1593	292	22	0
Moderate (1 to 3 years)	1401	347	24	7
Experienced	1551	393	51	17
Unknown	1710	449	83	23
Month of Year				
January	196	18	2	2
February	186	43	2	2
March	261	56	10	3
April	361	32	11	0
May	782	51	19	1
June	941	61	15	0
July	985	231	28	3
August	931	159	26	5
September	1098	61	15	4
October	373	30	14	1
November	169	11	3	0
December	81	21	2	1
Unknown	12	1	5	0
Type of Injury/Illness (Data since 1984)				
Fracture	938	178	5	6
Laceration	505	63	3	2
Abrasion	250	68	24	3
Bruise	323	69	33	2
Sprain/strain	223	24	26	3
Concussion	174	21	7	1
Hypothermia	129	14	5	0
Frostbite	95	9	4	0
Dislocation	90	10	1	1
Puncture	33	9	4	2

	1951–00 USA	1959–00 CAN.	2001 USA	2001 CAN.
Type of Injury/Illness (Data since 1984), cont.				
Acute Mountain Sickness	27	0	9	0
HAPE	56	0	6	0
HACE	19	0	1	0
Other[5]	222	36	18	1
None	165	76	0	0

N.B. Some accidents happen when climbers are at the top or bottom of a route, not climbing. They may be setting up a belay or rappel or are just not anchored when they fall.

[1] These illnesses, which led directly or indirectly to the accident, included: HAPE (3), HACE, internal bleeding—previous history of G.I. bleeds, exhaustion—unfit and de-hydrated, frostbite—inadequate footwear, stranded because of twisted knee—strained ACL, heart attack (one U.S., one Canada), transient ischemic attack (TIA).

[2] This includes rappelling off the end of the rope, anchor(s) inadequate, lowering a climber (from above or below).

[3] This category was set up originally for ski mountaineering. Backcountry touring or snowshoeing incidents—even if one gets avalanched—are not included in the data

[4] These included: inadequate instruction (3), caught ski tip on descent—heavy pack, failure to descend at first signs of AMS (4), foothold/handhold broke off (7), miscom-munication, dislodged rock which then broke rope, party dislodged rock and did not warn party below, inattention (2), guide book error, lost equipment.

[5] These included: rope burns on hands from rappelling or belaying improperly (3), internal bleeding (3), pneumothorax (2), hemothorax (2), strained ACL, pulmonary contusion, blindness caused by head injury from rock hitting forehead, ruptured Achilles tendon, collapsed lung, burns from lightning.

(Editor's Note: Under the category "other," many of the particular items will have been re-corded under a general category. For example, the climber who dislodges a rock that falls on another climber would be coded as Falling Rock/Object, or the climber who has a hand hold come loose and falls would also be coded as Fall On Rock.)

MOUNTAIN RESCUE UNITS IN NORTH AMERICA
**Denotes team fully certified—Technical Rock,
Snow & Ice, Wilderness Search;
S, R, SI = certified partially in Search, Rock, and/or Snow & Ice

ALASKA
ALASKA MOUNTAIN RESCUE GROUP. PO Box 241102, Anchorage,
AK 99524. www.amrg.org
DENALI NATIONAL PARK SAR. PO Box 588, Talkeetna, AK 99676.
Dena_talkeetna@nps.gov
US ARMY ALASKAN WARFARE TRAINING CENTER. #2900 501 Second
St., APO AP 96508

ARIZONA
APACHE RESCUE TEAM. PO Box 100, St. Johns, AZ 85936
ARIZONA DEPARTMENT OF PUBLIC SAFETY AIR RESCUE. Phoenix,
Flagstaff, Tucson, Kingman, AZ
ARIZONA DIVISION OF EMERGENCY SERVICES. Phoenix, AZ
GRAND CANYON NATIONAL PARK RESCUE TEAM. PO Box 129,
Grand Canyon, AZ 86023
****CENTRAL ARIZONA MOUNTAIN RESCUE TEAM/ MARICOPA
COUNTY SHERIFF'S OFFICE MR.** PO Box 4004 Phoenix, AZ 85030.
www.mcsomr.org
SEDONA FIRE DISTRICT SPECIAL OPERATIONS RESCUE TEAM.
2860 Southwest Dr., Sedona, AZ 86336. ropes@sedona.net
****SOUTHERN ARIZONA RESCUE ASSN/ PIMA COUNTY SHERIFF'S
OFFICE.** PO Box 12892, Tucson, AZ 85732.
http://hambox.theriver.com/sarci/sara01.html

CALIFORNIA
****ALTADENA MOUNTAIN RESCUE TEAM.** 780 E. Altadena Dr., Altadena,
CA 91001. www.altadenasheriffs.org/rescue/amrt.html
****BAY AREA MOUNTAIN RESCUE TEAM.** PO Box 19184, Stanford,
CA 94309. bamru@hooked.net
CALIFORNIA OFFICE OF EMERGENCY SERVICES. 2800 Meadowview
Rd., Sacramento, CA. 95832. warning.center@oes.ca.gov
****CHINA LAKE MOUNTAIN RESCUE GROUP.** PO Box 2037, Ridgecrest,
CA 93556. www.clmrg.org
****INYO COUNTY SHERIFF'S POSSE SAR.** PO Box 982, Bishop, CA 93514.
inyocosar@juno.com
JOSHUA TREE NATIONAL PARK SAR. 74485 National Monument Drive,
Twenty Nine Palms, CA 92277. patrick_suddath@nps.gov
****LOS PADRES SAR TEAM.** PO Box 6602, Santa Barbara, CA 93160-6602
****MALIBU MOUNTAIN RESCUE TEAM.** PO Box 222, Malibu, CA 90265.
www.mmrt.org
****MONTROSE SAR TEAM.** PO Box 404, Montrose, CA 91021

**RIVERSIDE MOUNTAIN RESCUE UNIT. PO Box 5444, Riverside,
CA 92517. www.rmru.org   rmru@bigfoot.com
SAN BERNARDINO COUNTY SHERIFF'S CAVE RESCUE TEAM.
655 E. Third St. San Bernardino, CA 92415
www.sbsd-vfu.org/units/SAR/SAR203/sar203_1.htm
**SAN BERNARDINO COUNTY SO/ WEST VALLEY SAR.
13843 Peyton Dr., Chino Hills, CA 91709.
**SAN DIEGO MOUNTAIN RESCUE TEAM. PO Box 81602, San Diego,
CA 92138. www.sdmrt.org
**SAN DIMAS MOUNTAIN RESCUE TEAM. PO Box 35, San Dimas,
CA 91773
**SANTA CLARITA VALLEY SAR / L.A.S.O. 23740 Magic Mountain Parkway,
Valencia, CA 91355. http://members.tripod.com/scvrescue/
SEQUOIA-KINGS CANYON NATIONAL PARK RESCUE TEAM.
Three Rivers, CA 93271
**SIERRA MADRE SAR. PO Box 24, Sierra Madre, CA 91025.
www.mra.org/smsrt.html
**VENTURA COUNTY SAR. 2101 E. Olson Rd, Thousand Oaks, CA 91362.
www.vcsar.org
YOSEMITE NATIONAL PARK RESCUE TEAM. PO Box 577-SAR,
Yosemite National Park, CA 95389

COLORADO
**ALPINE RESCUE TEAM. PO Box 934, Evergreen, CO 80439.
www.heart-beat-of-evergreen.com/alpine/alpine.html
COLORADO GROUND SAR. 2391 Ash St, Denver, CO 80222.
www.coloradowingcap.org/CGSART/Default.htm
**CRESTED BUTTE SAR. PO Box 485, Crested Butte, CO 81224
DOUGLAS COUNTY SEARCH AND RESCUE. PO Box 1102, Castle Rock,
CO 80104. www.dcsarco.org info@dcsarco.org
**EL PASO COUNTY SAR. 3950 Interpark Dr, Colorado Springs,
CO 80907-9028. www.epcsar.org
ELDORADO CANYON STATE PARK. PO Box B, Eldorado Springs,
CO 80025
**GRAND COUNTY SAR. Box 172, Winter Park, CO 80482
**LARIMER COUNTY SAR. 1303 N. Shields St., Fort Collins, CO 80524.
www.fortnet.org/LCSAR/ lcsar@co.larimer.co.us
**MOUNTAIN RESCUE ASPEN. 630 W. Main St, Aspen, CO 81611.
www.mountainrescueaspen.org
PARK COUNTY SAR, CO. PO Box 721, Fairplay, CO 80440
ROCKY MOUNTAIN NATIONAL PARK RESCUE TEAM.
Estes Park, CO 80517
**ROCKY MOUNTAIN RESCUE GROUP. PO Box Y, Boulder, CO 80306.
www.colorado.edu/StudentGroups/rmrg/ rmrg@colorado.edu
ROUTT COUNTY SAR. PO Box 772837, Steamboat Springs, CO 80477.
RCSAR@co.routt.co.us
**SUMMIT COUNTY RESCUE GROUP. PO Box 1794, Breckenridge,
CO 80424

**VAIL MOUNTAIN RESCUE GROUP. PO Box 1597, Vail, CO 81658.
http://sites.netscape.net/vailmra/homepage vmrg@vail.net
**WESTERN STATE COLLEGE MOUNTAIN RESCUE TEAM.
Western State College Union, Gunnison, CO 81231. org_mrt@western.edu

IDAHO
**BONNEVILLE COUNTY SAR. 605 N. Capital Ave, Idaho Falls, ID 83402.
www.srv.net/~jrcase/bcsar.html
**IDAHO MOUNTAIN SAR. PO Box 741, Boise, ID 83701. www.imsaru.org
rsksearch@aol.com

MAINE
ACADIA NATIONAL PARK SAR. Bar Harbor, Maine

MARYLAND
**MARYLAND SAR GROUP. 5434 Vantage Point Road, Columbia, MD 21044.
Peter_McCabe@Ed.gov

MONTANA
GLACIER NATIONAL PARK SAR. PO Box 423, Glacier National Park, West
Glacier, MT 59936
NORTHWEST MONTANA REGIONAL SAR ASSN. c/o Flat County SO,
800 S. Main, Kalispell, MT 59901
**WESTERN MONTANA MOUNTAIN RESCUE TEAM. University of
Montana, University Center—Rm 105 Missoula, MT 59812

NEVADA
**LAS VEGAS METRO PD SAR. 4810 Las Vegas Blvd., South Las Vegas,
NV 89119. www.lvmpdsar.com

NEW MEXICO
**ALBUQUERQUE MOUNTAIN RESCUE COUNCIL.
PO Box 53396, Albuquerque, NM 87153. www.abq.com/amrc/ albrescu@swcp.com

NEW HAMPSHIRE
APPALACHIAN MOUNTAIN CLUB. Pinkham Notch Camp, Gorham,
  NH 03581
MOUNTAIN RESCUE SERVICE. PO Box 494, North Conway, NH 03860

NEW YORK
76 SAR. 243 Old Quarry Rd., Feura Bush, NY 12067
NY STATE FOREST RANGERS. 50 Wolf Rd., room 440C, Albany, NY 12233

OREGON
CORVALLIS MOUNTAIN RESCUE UNIT. PO Box 116, Corvallis, OR 97339. www.cmrv.peak.org
(S, R) **DESCHUTES COUNTY SAR.** 63333 West Highway 20, Bend, OR 97701
EUGENE MOUNTAIN RESCUE. PO Box 20, Eugene, OR 97440
HOOD RIVER CRAG RATS RESCUE TEAM. 2880 Thomsen Rd., Hood River, OR 97031
PORTLAND MOUNTAIN RESCUE. PO Box 5391, Portland, OR 97228. www.pmru.org info@pmru.org

PENNSYLVANNIA
ALLEGHENY MOUNTAIN RESCUE GROUP. c/o Mercy Hospital, 1400 Locust, Pittsburgh, PA 15219. www.asrc.net/amrg
WILDERNESS EMERGENCY STRIKE TEAM. 11 North Duke Street, Lancaster, PA 17602. www.west610.org

UTAH
DAVIS COUNTY SHERIFF'S SAR. PO Box 800, Farmington, UT 84025. www.dcsar.org
ROCKY MOUNTAIN RESCUE DOGS. 3353 S. Main #122, Salt Lake City, UT 84115
SALT LAKE COUNTY SHERIFF'S SAR. 4474 South Main St., Murray, UT 84107
SAN JUAN COUNTY EMERGENCY SERVICES. PO Box 9, Monticello, UT 84539
UTAH COUNTY SHERRIF'S SAR. PO Box 330, Provo, UT 84603. ucsar@utah.uswest.net
WEBER COUNTY SHERIFF'S MOUNTAIN RESCUE. 745 Nancy Dr, Ogden, UT 84403. http://planet.weber.edu/mru
ZION NATIONAL PARK SAR. Springdale, UT 84767

VERMONT
STOWE HAZARDOUS TERRAIN EVACUATION. P.O. Box 291, Stowe, VT 05672. www.stowevt.org/htt/

VIRGINIA
AIR FORCE RESCUE COORDINATION CENTER. Suite 101, 205 Dodd Building, Langley AFB, VA 23665. www2.acc.af.mil/afrcc/ airforce.rescue@usa.net

WASHINGTON STATE
BELLINGHAM MOUNTAIN RESCUE COUNCIL. PO Box 292, Bellingham, WA 98225
CENTRAL WASHINGTON MOUNTAIN RESCUE COUNCIL. PO Box 2663, Yakima, WA 98907. www.nwinfo.net/~cwmr/ cwmr@nwinfo.net